CONTENTS

Henry Royce, the son of a miller, was born in 1863 at Alwalton, near Peterborough. Aged nine when his father died, his mother and aunt brought him up in the best way they were able but nevertheless it was necessary for him to sell newspapers to supplement the family income. At the age of twelve, having had just three years of schooling, Henry began work as a telegraph boy before taking an apprenticeship with the Great Northern Railway. Financial hardships prevented him from completing his apprenticeship; he undertook a variety of engineering and electrical jobs, all of which placed him in good stead when he established his own business manufacturing electrical equipment.

Charles Stewart Rolls, third son of Lord and Lady Llangattock, was born in 1877. He was brought up at the family home at The Hendre, Monmouthshire, attended Eton and, at the age of seventeen, visited France where he acquired a Peugeot, his first motor car. One of Britain's earliest motoring enthusiasts, he did much to further the cause of motoring and was instrumental in popularising the sport of motor racing.

As well as showing prowess in motoring, Rolls was also an accomplished balloonist and later became a recognised aviator. It was his love of the automobile, however, which determined that he would establish his own business selling motor cars to those daring enough to sample the pleasures of car ownership. With a showroom in Mayfair and a workshop in nearby Fulham, he sold only the best cars of the period which included, among others, Peugeots and Panhards. Rolls was introduced to Royce in 1904 and it was that meeting, at the Midland Hotel in Manchester, that led to the eventual establishment of Rolls-Royce.

INTRODUCTION

No single make of car can have enjoyed the charisma and reputation of either Rolls-Royce or Bentley, the former having had bestowed upon it the accolade the 'Best Car in the World' and the latter being recognised as the 'Silent Sports Car'. Together, the two marques may now be synonymous but it was not always so; Rolls-Royce pre-dates Bentley by some fifteen years and, in the beginning, Henry Royce had built his first motor car before there was any association with the Hon. Charles Stewart Rolls.

The backgrounds of Rolls and Royce were so very different that any future alliance between the two could be considered most unlikely. C.S. Rolls was born into the aristocracy while Henry Royce, fourteen years his senior, experienced hardship in his early life and received little in the way of schooling. While Rolls had been brought up on the family estate in Monmouthshire, later attending Eton, Royce was selling newspapers in London.

The paths of the two, however, proved not to be totally removed: Rolls fell in love with the motor car when the automobile was in its infancy, by which time Royce, having been apprenticed in the railway industry, was following a tortuous career which spanned both engineering and electricity. Rolls acquired his first motor car in France and brought it to England where he helped pioneer the art of motoring. Less than a decade later, Royce, having established his own engineering company in Cooke Street, Manchester, had also succumbed to the pleasures of motoring. He had purchased a car, a Decauville, in 1902. Royce's thoroughness and attention to detail led him not only to disassemble the machine and rebuild it to his own exacting standards, but to construct a vehicle of his own which, in engineering terms, was superior to any other of the period. Thus the first Royce motor car was born.

By the time Henry Royce had built his first motor car, C.S. Rolls had established his own business with a showroom in London's fashionable Mayfair and workshops at Fulham from which he succeeded in selling motor cars, mainly to the aristocracy and successful businesspeople. He was also a prominent contender in the brand-new sport of motor racing and achieved notoriety by winning, in 1900, the Thousand Miles Reliability Trial, the first motoring event of its kind to be held.

Two men, Ernest Claremont and Henry Edmunds, provided the link between Rolls and Royce; Claremont, Royce's business partner, was also a director of W.T. Glover & Company, a manufacturer of electrical wiring in Manchester, along with Edmunds who, as another pioneering motorist, was a friend of C.S. Rolls. Rolls had already expressed a wish to promote British cars rather than the Panhards and Peugeots with which he normally dealt and, as Edmunds knew he was also looking for a suitable machine to which he could associate his name, arranged for the two to meet.

That momentous meeting took place at the Midland Hotel, Manchester, on 4 May 1904. The two men, despite their differing backgrounds, got on well and Rolls was impressed with

Royce's car. Such was the convivial atmosphere that an agreement was quickly reached whereby Rolls would sell all the cars that Royce could produce; most importantly, however, the liaison led to Charles Rolls and Henry Royce agreeing in December 1904 to the cars carrying their joint names.

Rolls-Royce motor cars quickly built up a reputation for quality and craftsmanship. The person responsible for publicising the cars' virtues was Claude Johnson (often referred to as the 'hyphen between Rolls and Royce'), a senior member in Rolls's company, but undoubtedly it was Rolls himself who championed its robustness and reliability. He achieved this by driving the car to victory in the 1906 Isle of Man Tourist Trophy at an average speed of nearly 40mph. The early history of Rolls-Royce continued to be graced by such motor cars as the Silver Ghost, possibly the most famous and respected of all models; the Twenty was introduced in 1921 alongside the Silver Ghost and was continued until 1929 when it was replaced by the 20/25 which became the best-selling Rolls-Royce during the inter-war years.

In 1931 Rolls-Royce acquired Bentley, an equally famous British motor car since 1919 when W.O. Bentley formed a company to produce sporting vehicles from premises at Cricklewood in north London. Bentley was the doyen of Brooklands, in Surrey, the first and most famous of all purpose-built motor racing circuits, and the marque, synonymous with the exploits of Tim Birkin and the Bentley Boys, is seen as the epitome of the vintage sports car.

Before the Second World War the diversity of Rolls-Royce and Bentley chassis styles indicated that some rationalisation was necessary if the company was to survive a changing and more competitive motor industry. Post-war car production incorporated not only the rationalisation measures devised in the late thirties but standardisation too. The demise of the major part of the coachbuilding industry necessitated the use of pressed steel car bodies, designed in the Rolls-Royce idiom but manufactured in much the same way as those intended for more popular makes of vehicle. Of course, there was no loss in quality and the cars of the early post-war period proved to be every bit as good as their predecessors.

In the early sixties, the directors of Rolls-Royce had to make some far-reaching decisions: it was evident that the company, in order to compete in a motor industry comprising a new breed of young and demanding customers, would need to produce motor cars in far greater numbers than before. The capacity to build cars in the quantities envisaged without loss of quality was simply not possible using existing methods and, as a result, rationalisation evolved to incorporate unitary construction techniques.

When introduced in 1965, the Silver Shadow and its stablemate, the Bentley T-Series, represented a huge leap forward in technology as far as Rolls-Royce was concerned and proved to be the most radical model in the company's long and illustrious history. It was, of course, just as much a Rolls-Royce as any other; not only was it built in vast numbers compared to its predecessors but the Silver Shadow laid the foundations on which the existence of the marque would depend for generations.

The legacy of Henry Royce, which dictates the most careful attention to detail in every aspect of the cars bearing his name, lives on, and it is this which makes the Rolls-Royce and the Bentley very special. There are certainly cars that have been more expensive, faster and, arguably, as well engineered; none, however, receive such admiration.

Malcolm Bobbitt, Cumbria, 1997

ORIGINS

Many hours were spent in perfecting the prototype cars and only when Royce was satisfied they were ready to be road-tested were the bodies fitted to the chassis. This very early photograph shows the first car (with a Manchester trade registration number) completed and ready to be tried out by a rather apprehensive-looking young man who is thought to be one of the draughtsmen. It should be noted that the radiator shape is quite different from that which came to be the visible hallmark of Rolls-Royce cars as, at the time, there was no association between Henry Royce and C.S. Rolls.

INTRODUCTION

There is some conjecture about whether Henry Royce determinedly entered motor car production or if the venture was arrived at accidentally. Royce's fascination for anything mechanical certainly made him an ideal candidate for motor manufacture, but it does appear that his first encounter with motor transport was anything but planned.

After establishing an electrical manufacturing business with Ernest Claremont at Cooke Street, Manchester, long hours spent at the work bench and overwork brought about a period of ill-health which was cured only by a long holiday visiting his wife's relations in South Africa. Returning home, Royce's doctor suggested he acquire a quadricycle, which was not so much a car as a couple of bicycles joined together with a feeble engine. Nevertheless, Royce achieved immense enjoyment from the machine which, it appears, was quite unsuitable for the road on account of its brakes which were rendered useless by oil seeping on to them from the engine.

Compared to France, the motor industry in Britain got off to a shaky and late start with only a few cars running at the turn of the century. Perhaps the experience with the quadricycle whetted his appetite for motoring for, in 1902, Royce purchased a second-hand French Decauville. One thing is certain: Henry Royce made sure that he kept abreast of all engineering developments and would have known of the progress car manufacturers were making in France and elsewhere.

As well as expanding his electrical interests, Royce also built up a business manufacturing cranes; the enterprise was successful and he even managed to export some equipment to Japan. That the crane business eventually went into decline may have caused Royce to seek alternative manufacturing areas and, anticipating that it would only be a matter of time before the motor car flourished in Britain, he may have felt confident of eventual success. In any case, it is known that Royce, keen to learn exactly how the Decauville worked, took the car to bits and rebuilt it in the manner he thought correct.

The early years of the century therefore found Henry Royce experimenting with three prototype cars based loosely on the Decauville. The comparisons between these and the French car were far from close: Royce's meticulous engineering ensured that the Cooke Street cars were superior; they were also preferable to almost anything else that was available in Britain at that time. The question remains, however – was Royce biding his time to find an associate willing to work with him in the car manufacturing industry?

Along with his business partner, Ernest Claremont, Royce established his electrical business manufacturing bell sets in premises at Cooke Street, Manchester, in 1884. This picture was, however, taken at a much later date, possibly in the thirties.

This car, a Decauville, is similar to the one that Royce purchased in 1902. It is reported that Royce's experiences with the car were not exactly happy but his engineering expertise enabled him not only to take the car apart and rebuild it completely, but to build a car of his own with many improvements.

Royce decided to experiment with car production by building three prototype machines, the first of which is shown here in chassis form. It is evident that a radiator cooling fan is absent and it is generally thought that this was never fitted. The 2-cylinder engine, rated at 10hp, incorporated a valve arrangement with an overhead inlet and side exhaust. Known as the 'F-head', this type of valve layout was later used on post-1946 cars and adopted by the Rover company around the same time.

Ernest Claremont was allocated one of the three prototype cars for his personal use. Similar in style to this car, the vehicle is pictured outside the Cooke Street entrance of Royce Limited. It appears the car has recently been put through its paces, judging by the extent of mud splashes on the front wheel-arches and rear guards, and might suggest it had endured its first trials which were carried out on 1 April 1904.

The second Royce car, with Eric Platford at the wheel, is on test in the Peak District. This car was entered for the Slideslip Trials, an event organised by the Automobile Club in the third week of April 1904. Included was a day's reliability trial which saw nine cars leaving London's Piccadilly for Margate via Dartford, Gravesend and Canterbury, a round trip of 145 miles. The Slideslip Trials lasted a week, in which time the cars completed 850 miles. Of the Royce car, a correspondent of the *Morning Post* recalled the car's excellent running, whether on the level or negotiating steep hills.

Henry Royce's wife, Minnie, was a source of constant encouragement and support to him. Here she is shown at the wheel of an early car at Brae Cottage, the family home in Knutsford, some time during 1904. The lady passenger is said to be a Mrs Smith; the pair seem to be posing for the photograph, which is probably why both ladies appear not to be too concerned at the thought of taking the car on the road.

Commander James Percy, one of Britain's pioneering motorists, is obviously having difficulties with a pneumatic tyre on one of the prototype Royce cars. Punctures were experienced with some regularity by motorists during this period, which is not surprising considering the condition of the road surface shown in this picture.

The car's body style is different from other Royce vehicles and it appears this was fitted especially for the Paris show where the car was demonstrated. During those formative years Royce had a habit of switching around both bodies and registration plates between cars which makes identification tricky.

Illustrated here is the vast interior of Rolls' workshops at Lillie Hall, Fulham, *c.* 1905, after Rolls and Royce had reached an agreement whereby Rolls would sell Royce's cars, and evidenced by the fact that a number of Rolls-Royce machines can be seen. The vehicles parked in the premises are varied, but certainly Panhards are stocked and it is known Rolls was agent for Mors and the Belgian Minerva. At the turn of the century French cars were considered among the best available in Britain; Rolls progressed from his initial Peugeot to Panhards and it was in the latter that he took the then Duke and Duchess of York (later King George V and Queen Mary) for their inaugural car ride.

Rolls was clearly impressed with Henry Royce's car and he can be seen at the wheel of the first Royce in August 1904. Alongside Rolls is HRH the Duke of Connaught; standing at the front of the car is Lord Brabazon of Tara (at the time he was J.T.C. Moore-Brabazon), while at the rear is a member of the Motor Volunteer Corps. Pictured at Folkestone, the party was conducting a tour of inspection of the south coast defences.

Before contemplating motor car production Henry Royce had manufactured electrical equipment and cranes. As this part of his business was in decline, he had space to spare in his works; this enabled him to build his prototype cars. The fitting shop at Cooke Street evolved into a hive of activity, as is suggested by this early photograph. The picture was taken around August 1905, after the Rolls-Royce agreement.

PIONEERING DAYS

Among the first of Rolls-Royce's customers was Dr K. Gillies who is seen at the wheel of his car suitably attired for contemporary motoring. C.S. Rolls was instrumental in selling Royce's cars; not only was he highly respected but his activities in motor sport allowed him to publicise those cars with which he was associated. Much of the motor sport in Britain was at the time organised by what was to become the RAC and the success of the events that were held around the country was attributed to Claude Johnson, the organisation's secretary. The fact that Royces and Rolls-Royces performed favourably in motor sport added to the cars' reputation.

INTRODUCTION

Completion of the first Royce car, along with the many hours of tedious testing, mostly based on trial and error, could have ended in disaster for Henry Royce and his team of pioneering mechanics. The fact that the first road trial of the prototype was quite satisfactory illustrates the fastidious attention to detail devoted not only to this project but to all Royce's ventures.

It has been recorded that when the first Royce car drove out of the Cooke Street works with Henry Royce at the wheel, he was accompanied by the full noise and enthusiasm of the workforce who banged and rattled anything and everything in sight – such was the event which gave birth to one of the world's greatest motor cars. Royce, however, was more quietly indulgent than those at their workbenches; he drove the fifteen miles home to Brae Cottage at Knutsford to show his wife the product of his and his employees' labours.

Whether Royce, the car builder, knew of C.S. Rolls's existence is unknown, but he certainly would have known what was going on in the fledgling motor industry as, with all matters concerning engineering, he kept abreast of all the latest events and technology. As for Rolls, who was at the industry's forefront, he was certainly aware of Royce; his associate, Henry Edmunds, director of W.T. Glover, the electrical wiring manufacturer and supplier to Royce, made it his business to acquaint him with the engineer's motor-car development. Indeed, Rolls had asked Edmunds to keep him informed of any eventuality that might result in his forming an association with a particular car to which he could safely apply his name.

It was through the efforts of Edmunds that the meeting between Rolls and Royce came about. Rolls wanted Royce to meet him in London; Royce refused, and Rolls, on account of the fame of Royce's car, was persuaded to travel to Manchester, where the meeting took place at the Midland Hotel on 4 May 1904.

Two agreements followed that memorable meeting: the first stipulated that Rolls would act as agent for Royce's cars; the second confirmed that they would be known as Rolls-Royces. C.S. Rolls's prestigious standing in the motor industry was enough to ensure the cars' high profile and Royce did not seem at all perturbed that the manufacturer's name followed Rolls's.

During the formative years of Rolls-Royce, the cars from Cooke Street received no higher accolade than that of winning the 1906 Tourist Trophy, having already achieved second position the previous year.

Following the agreement to sell Royce cars under the joint name of Rolls-Royce, two cars were built using the style of radiator of the first Royce cars. It was not until the third Rolls-Royce that the now-familiar Grecian-styled radiator was introduced. It has been suggested that the style originated on the Norfolk car (built from 1904 to 1905), but other accounts suggest that it was Claude Johnson who advised the cars should carry an impressively designed radiator.

Another view of Dr Gillies; the now-familiar bonnet shape is fully evident, as is the radiator. The car depicted is similar to that advertised in *The Autocar* of 17 December 1904; with Park Phaeton body, the selling price was £436.

In 1905 S. Gammell, of Countesswells House, Bieldside, Aberdeenshire, purchased this 10hp car, registered SU 13. In 1946 after 100,000 miles, the car was donated to Rolls-Royce. At the wheel of the car, when it was received by Rolls-Royce, is Harry Fleck, once C.S. Rolls's chauffeur. Harry's long service with both C.S. Rolls & Co. and Rolls-Royce has been well documented and at least one other picture of him at the wheel of a Rolls-Royce in the early 1900s is included elsewhere in this book.

One of three remaining examples of the 10hp, this historic photograph is significant in that the car originally sold to S. Gammell in 1905 can be seen alongside one of the very first Rolls-Royces to have been built. Carrying the registration AX 148, the 10hp is included in the Science Museum's collection of motor vehicles. The date of this photograph is unknown but from the styling of the Morris and Ford Prefect cars visible beyond the gates, a good guess is that it may have been around the mid-fifties.

The 10hp heading a queue of cars at a motoring event during the mid-fifties. Apart from the cars following the Rolls-Royce, note the relative absence of traffic on what is clearly a major road. In 1905 there were no luxuries such as flashing direction indicators (although the first semaphore-type had been seen that year on a German car) and the front passenger in the car, who is Raymond Baxter, the celebrated broadcaster and journalist, is nevertheless quite happy to indicate a left turn!

Major Rushton was so pleased with his 2-cylinder 10hp Rolls-Royce that he wrote to C.S. Rolls & Co. to advise of his great satisfaction. The photograph has an eerie quality about it which has been caused by the fact that the front part of the car has been drawn or 'touched in'.

There can be few photographs of early motoring that are as evocative as this. Joseph and Mary Blamires, together with their daughter, Emma, are pictured taking a drive in their 2-cylinder 10hp Rolls-Royce. When this picture was taken, motoring was still considered a recreation almost exclusively enjoyed by the wealthy and the aristocracy.

Above: Henry Royce lent Eric Platford and his bride an early Rolls-Royce for their honeymoon. A trainee with Royce Limited, Platford eventually became Chief Tester. Below: Dr Warre, headmaster of Eton where C.S. Rolls received his schooling, was presented with this desirable motor car by old Etonians on the occasion of his retirement in 1905. Built on a 15hp chassis with Phaeton de luxe bodywork, the Brougham top was removable so that the vehicle could be used as an open carriage.

Only a single 15hp Rolls-Royce has survived; registered SD 661, it originally carried the registration number LC 2782 and was the second 15hp 3-cylinder car to leave the Cooke Street works. Used initially as a demonstration car, it was sold on to Thomas Dundas of Northallerton, Yorkshire, but the car was sold to Countess Loudoun of Ayrshire on the death of Dundas only a year after he had acquired it. Eventually sold by the countess, who could not get on with the car, it was bought by Douglas Dick who used it continuously until 1920. Happily the car has been restored and C.W. Morton, the authority on Rolls-Royce cars, can be seen refitting the engine (above) and (below) at the controls. Alongside Morton is Jimmy Chadwick, who was once an apprentice at Cooke Street.

In similar style to Dr Warre's car is a 20hp with a Double Brougham body; the car, it appears, was highly regarded when displayed in Paris, where it was awarded a bronze medal. After the Paris show, the car was acquired by A.H. Briggs of Harrogate, Yorkshire; a businessman, Briggs was also a keen motorist who advocated motor sport and, not surprisingly, was a friend of C.S. Rolls and later became a director of Rolls-Royce.

The Rolls-Royce Legalimit was something of an enigma; the engine, an early example of a V8, was the most advanced product of Rolls-Royce at the time of its introduction in 1905/6. For all its size, however, the 3,500cc unit was designed to propel the car at no more than the 20mph speed limit which was in force at the time. Note how low the engine sits in the chassis, a feature which made it ideal for under-floor fitting in a subsequent model which was designed as a town car, the motor being invisible. The vehicle depicted in this photograph is the only one of its type to have been built; it was sold to Baron Northcliffe in 1906.

During August 1905, C.S. Rolls was conducting a group of French naval officers to Windsor when this photograph was taken. The car is a 30hp, identifiable not only by the sheer size of the vehicle but by the forward position of the radiator. The experience of being driven in a Rolls-Royce must have been quite novel for the Frenchmen who were probably rather more used to Panhards and Mors. As an aside, C.S. Rolls was quite familiar with driving on French roads, even at this date; before he became associated with Royce cars, he had driven from Paris to England in an 8hp 4-cylinder Panhard which was then the last word in technology.

One of the first events in which Rolls-Royce cars gained prominence was the Tourist Trophy (TT); although C.S. Rolls failed to finish in the 1905 Isle of Man race, his car, nevertheless, was subject to much consternation. Questions were raised as to the car's suitability to start on, and climb, steep gradients, and to quell any further argument Claude Johnson arranged for a series of spectacular events to be staged. After a trial over a half mile stretch of road in London's Mall, two cars were taken to the south London suburb of Sydenham where they were subjected to Jasper Road's 1 in 6 gradient. With Claude Johnson at the wheel of a 20hp machine, he started the car on the steep hill with as many as nine passengers aboard and carried on until the top of the hill was reached. There was, it appears, no cause for further controversy.

This evocative picture was found in Rolls-Royce's archives and shows Percy Northey with C.S. Rolls aboard the 20hp car which was entered for the 1905 Isle of Man TT event. The picture is in recognition of Northey's considerable feat of covering 208.5 miles at an average speed of 33.75mph and attaining a fuel consumption of no less than 24.8mpg.

This photograph is not what it seems! These cars are neither Royces nor Rolls-Royces; the first and third are Alldays, which adopted a similar radiator styling to that of the Rolls-Royce. For all it is a very misleading photograph, it is nevertheless most evocative of motor sport during those early days of motoring.

The 20hp was built in two guises, as a Light 20 and a Heavy 20. It is the latter which the young
H. Fergusson-Wood is attempting to steer; the car left Cooke Street on 18 October 1905 and was
originally sold to Wellington Williams of Mayfield, Sussex, the young man's uncle. The scale of the
bodywork is quite obvious from the size of the young would-be motorist; at the time of purchase this
would have been the ultimate in motor cars.

The Heavy 20 was so-called not because of the chassis weight but because it could support heavier
coachwork than might otherwise have been fitted. The first chassis in the series was fitted with a Roi des
Belges touring body and it is this vehicle that was supplied to the committee of the Automobile Club
(RAC) to oversee the Gordon Bennett race trials on the Isle of Man as an official car. Claude Johnson,
who was very impressed with the car's performance, had already given it the name Grey Ghost, which it
retained for the rest of its life. In this illustration, Eric Platford, at the wheel, is sitting alongside one of
the Manx race officials outside the entrance to Glen Helen in May 1905.

Lady Llangattock, C.S. Rolls's mother, prepares to take a ride in a 30hp 6-cylinder Rolls-Royce. The location is The Hendre, the family home in Monmouthshire, and although the occasion is undated it is likely to have been around 1905–6.

The lady passenger who appears suitably attired for a drive on what seems to be a pleasant spring day, is the Hon. Mrs A.E.(May) Assheton-Harbord, for whom the car was supplied in 1906. At the wheel of the 30hp 6-cylinder car is Harry Fleck of C.S. Rolls & Co., who was often called upon to drive both Mrs Assheton-Harbord and 'Charlie' Rolls ('Charlie' was used only behind his back) on their ballooning exploits. The balloons were kept at the Battersea Gas Works where the Short Brothers (of aviation fame) had a business which included manufacturing, maintaining and filling them.

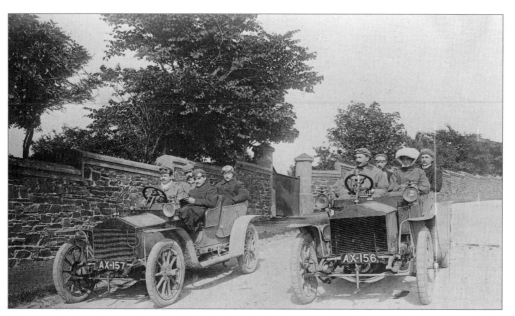

There can be few photographs more historic than this. It shows two Rolls-Royces, both 20hp 4-cylinder cars, preparing for the 1906 Isle of Man TT event. The picture was taken outside Woodlands, on the island at Douglas, where the TT races began. At the wheel of AX 157 is C.S. Rolls and alongside him Eric Platford; the two passengers in the rear are unknown. Percy Northey is driving AX 156 but his passengers have not been recorded, although one of the gentlemen is likely to be Durlacher, Northey's co-driver. Unfortunately the glass plate negative has become broken but it nevertheless portrays an excellent account of the two cars and occasion.

At the wheel of car no. 4 is C.S. Rolls, who is ready to take part in the 1906 Isle of Man TT event. Alongside Rolls is possibly Eric Platford, the clue to this being that he was sitting next to him in the same car the day before. Looking somewhat pensive, Rolls, who was a very competent mechanic, may well have been listening to the engine note and satisfying himself all was well, especially after the previous year's race when he was forced to withdraw following a gearbox failure. In the background, and to the left of Rolls's car, can be seen vehicle no. 5, this being AX 156 driven by Percy Northey.

C.S. Rolls's TT car is being refuelled before the start of the 1906 Isle of Man event. Rolls can be seen supervising the delivery of petrol which, at that period, was often referred to as 'benzoline' or 'benzine'. A principal supplier of benzine sold the spirit as 'petrol' and as no patent was taken out for the name, its use became universal. The activity around the filling point – note the petrol is referred to as Shell motor spirit – is very hectic and it appears that the fuel is being administered very carefully. The car driven by Percy Northey is clearly visible in the background and as he is not at the wheel it can only be supposed that he is involved with Rolls in the petrol delivery.

The 1906 TT event was held on 27 September (a Thursday) and consisted of four circuits of the course which started at Woodlands, Douglas, and continued via Peel to Ballaugh, Ramsey and over Snaefell before returning to Douglas. A total distance of 161 miles, fuel was rationed to 1 gallon per 22.54 miles. The race started at 9 a.m. and Rolls with Platford as his co-driver roared off in pursuit of the competing cars which included Darracqs, Berliets, Arrol-Johnston, Argyll, Bianchi and at least one Minerva. Northey, with a Lillie Hall mechanic by the name of Durlacher, driving AX 156, broke a spring on a bend and was forced to withdraw from the race; for Rolls and Platford, who were averaging 40mph and exceeding 50mph in places, the event was theirs and they crossed the finishing line in first position at 1.10 p.m.

Rolls, always a popular figure in motoring, won much acclaim for his success in the 1906 TT. Both Rolls and Platford were chaired at the winning post and with little doubt were the heroes of sportsmen and schoolboys alike. Always modest, Rolls awarded his victory not to himself or Platford but to Henry Royce: 'as I had nothing to do but sit there and wait until the car got to the finish the credit is obviously due to Mr Royce, the designer and builder'. Back at Cooke Street, Henry Royce was overjoyed but not as much as his employees who picked up their master and carried him around the works rejoicing. When the excitement was over he gave the workforce the rest of the day off (with pay) and went home quietly to tell his wife of the achievement.

Paris E. Singer, of sewing-machine fame, bought this, the last 15hp 3-cylinder model, in September 1907. It was reacquired by Rolls-Royce later in its life and it is shown here in company service at the Derby factory in 1913. Certain alterations were made to the car over the years; new dome-shaped mudguards have been fitted and the hood has been replaced with that of a twill variety instead of the original leatherette. When built, the car featured sliding doors and a hinged windscreen which fortunately have remained.

THE SILVER GHOST

The Silver Ghost is possibly the most instantly recognised car in the world. Representative of the 40/50hp model, the chassis of which was on display at the 1906 Olympia Motor Show, the car illustrated is actually the thirteenth to have been built and was used by C.S. Rolls as a company demonstration car. It became most famous, however, for two feats of endurance – first a 2,000-mile marathon publicity event and secondly for its performance during the 15,000-mile RAC-observed proving run which incorporated the 1907 Scottish Reliability Trial.

INTRODUCTION

The Silver Ghost was the name given to a particular car which was, in essence, the 40/50hp, the first model to appear from the newly formed Rolls-Royce Limited. Before the establishment of the new company, the cars of Henry Royce which had been sold through C.S. Rolls & Co. had already carried the R-R monogram, denoting the association between the two companies, and which now took on a new significance. The establishment of Rolls-Royce Limited came about on 16 March 1906 and the former C.S. Rolls showroom in Conduit Street and workshops at Lillie Hall, Fulham, were transferred to the new undertaking. As for Cooke Street, where Royce continued car manufacturing, that remained a separate entity.

The 40/50hp was unveiled during the autumn of 1906 at London's Olympia, where it caused a sensation among the motoring fraternity. Until the model's appearance, those interested in Royce and Rolls-Royce cars had become accustomed to the uniform engine policy which had produced not only the 10hp 2-cylinder but the 15hp 3-cylinder, 20hp 4-cylinder and 30hp 6-cylinder; for the 40/50hp, Royce had developed an entirely new engine of 7,036cc swept volume.

The car's endurance qualities were quickly recognised when the Silver Ghost left Bexhill-on-Sea in May 1907 on a 2,000 mile marathon which was supervised by the RAC and took in the proposed route of the Scottish Reliability Trial. A month later the Silver Ghost, having been stripped down to check for undue wear and tear, was entered for a gruelling 15,000-mile exercise which incorporated the Scottish event proper. The course was completed with ease: C.S. Rolls, Claude Johnson and Eric Platford, each sharing the driving, suffered only a single involuntary stop when the petrol tap shook itself into the closed position.

As for Cooke Street, production of cars had reached a level which the Manchester factory could no longer sustain. In seeking alternative premises, a site at Derby was eventually chosen where car production remained until the outbreak of the Second World War. For all the successes of the Silver Ghost and those cars associated with it, this period in the history of Rolls-Royce did have its tragedies: on 11 July 1910, C.S. Rolls was killed when his aeroplane suffered an in-flight structural failure at Bournemouth during a flying exhibition.

During its 15,000-mile endurance test in 1907, the Silver Ghost, registration AX 201 and pictured on the far left, is accompanied by three other 40/50hp cars at the Cat and Fiddle Inn near Buxton, Derbyshire. At the wheel of AX 201 is Claude Johnson; C.S. Rolls can be seen in the driving seat of the car alongside, AX 205. Note the differing body styles of all four cars; AX 205 has a different type of windscreen and the other two vehicles do not appear to have any screens at all.

The Silver Ghost in good company. Now a forceful means of publicity for Rolls-Royce, the car was reunited with the company when part-exchanged during the immediate post-war years for a new Bentley Mk VI. The car has now been completely restored and fully deserves the accolade bestowed upon it ninety years ago as the 'Best Car in the World'.

Pictured outside the Land's End Hotel around 1907/8, Henry Royce can be seen in the front passenger seat of a Silver Ghost. Royce was probably supervising one of the car's trials but who was actually about to drive is a mystery. One can presume it was either Eric Platford or Harry Fleck, but as the occasion of the photograph is also unclear it would be unwise to make such assumptions. The identity of the lady sitting in the rear is also uncertain.

A 15,000-mile endurance trial with nothing other than a petrol tap shaking itself shut is an impressive achievement by any standards. The fact that it took place as early as 1907 is even more remarkable. Claude Johnson, at the wheel of the Silver Ghost, is putting the car through its paces while competing in the Scottish Reliability Trials; beside him is C.S. Rolls.

In 1907 Silver Ghost broke the world record for a non-stop motor run in spectacular style. Organiser of the event was Claude Johnson, commercial managing director of Rolls-Royce, who is seen at the wheel of the car with C.S. Rolls, who shared the driving and is sitting at the rear of the car nearest the camera. Along with Claude Johnson and Rolls, the designated drivers were Eric Platford and 'Mechanician' Macready.

Here is the famous Rolls-Royce Silver Ghost, pictured arriving in Glasgow from London. Alongside is a 30hp White steam car which accompanied it for part of the route. Even today, driving the 400 miles between the two cities is a daunting prospect, but imagine doing this every day in 1907 in pursuit of the world record for a non-stop motor run over questionable roads with an absence of motorways. The two cars are obviously the subject of much attention and excitement and the occasion would no doubt have been immensely enjoyed by C.S. Rolls who can be seen at the wheel of the Silver Ghost. Note, incidentally, the size of the White steamer compared to that of the Rolls-Royce.

Claude Johnson was always keen to take advantage of any publicity and he can be seen at the wheel of Silver Phantom. It was in the Silver Ghost, as one of the car's designated drivers, that he participated in the record-breaking run of 1907 which, day after day, journeyed the 400 miles between London and Glasgow, taking the Scottish Reliability Trials en route. As well as the stamina displayed by the drivers, it was also a considerable achievement for the car and Royce's engineering.

This is a most odd photograph in as much as it was obviously intended for publicity use. By looking carefully it can be seen that the background has been obliterated and that another car, behind the Rolls-Royce, has been obscured. Nevertheless, it is a good picture of Claude Johnson, at the wheel of the car, and a superb portrayal of the road conditions of the era. Note the amount of dust and mud that accumulated along the car which, in reality, offered little in the way of protection.

The awesome prospect of taking any car across some of the most isolated country without metalled roads is aptly depicted in this photograph of a 40/50hp open tourer tackling a difficult stretch of terrain. While there is no indication as to the date of the photograph there is every suggestion it was taken much later than the Scottish Reliability Trials if the style of the driver's dress is anything to go by. The illustration does, of course, clearly express how rugged and well-engineered the Silver Ghost and 40/50hp cars were.

Rolls-Royce cars had attained for themselves an impressive reputation by the time this photograph was taken. Not only had the 20hp cars given a sparkling performance in the 1905 and 1906 TT events on the Isle of Man but the Silver Ghost had attained virtual legendary status within its own lifetime by ably enduring two marathon runs within a year. In this photograph, C.S. Rolls appears to be giving the crowd of spectators a thrill on a particularly difficult section of road while competing in the 1908 Scottish Reliability Trials with his Silver Rogue. Winning its class in the International Touring Car Trial – which included 200 laps of the newly opened Brooklands track near Weybridge, Surrey – the car later went on to complete 20 laps at the same circuit at a speed of a fraction under 66mph.

Cooke Street, the original home of Royce and Rolls-Royce cars, had become so limited in facilities that it was accepted a new factory would have to be found. After much searching the choice was either a 'greenfield' site at Leicester or Derby, with the latter, at Nightingale Road, being chosen due to the promise of cheap electrical power from Derby Corporation. Most of the negotiation was carried out by Claude Johnson but it was Henry Royce who saw to the design of the factory buildings. The factory was officially opened on 9 July 1908 by Lord Montagu of Beaulieu, another of Britain's pioneering motorists. Obviously a gala day, there is much for onlookers to see; note the queue of Rolls-Royces carrying dignatories. The leading car, the Silver Rogue driven by Eric Platford with Lord Montagu as passenger, is the same as that pictured while competing in the 1908 Scottish Trials on the previous page.

Henry Royce enjoys a little relaxation outside his home at Quarndon; by his side is his black Labrador dog, Rajah. In the picture also is a Silver Ghost which, for Rolls-Royce, was so successful. Some 7,876 Silver Ghost chassis were built over twenty years with production spanning three factories: Cooke Street, where the early cars were built, Derby, which produced the greatest output, and Springfield, Massachusetts, which supplied cars mainly for the American market.

The Silver Ghost may have won a reputation for rugged reliability but nothing can protect even a Rolls-Royce from the vagaries of a road accident. The car being towed away by a Daimler breakdown truck has been rendered little more than a mass of twisted metal and the question arises as to the severity of the crash. Undated, but clearly around the period of the First World War, the incident appears to have occurred in Kingston, south-west London. Judging by the petrol pump in the background, the picture may have been taken just as the Silver Ghost is being towed into the garage.

C.S. Rolls at the wheel of a Silver Ghost, named 'The Cookie', which was designed to carry his ballooning equipment. Rolls was, of course, an avid balloonist and even became noted as an aerial photographer. One of his most famous pictures is of the Eiffel Tower, taken on a visit to France. His ballooning activities led him to take more than a passing interest in aviation, the sport responsible for his untimely death.

C.S. Rolls's association with aviation is evident in this photograph which shows him in company with the Wright brothers, Horace Short and Griffith Brewer, in 1910. Rolls is at the wheel of a 40/50hp; beside him smoking a pipe is Horace Short, while Orville Wright is nearest the camera. Griffith Brewer (wearing the flat cap) helped to revive ballooning as a sport during the Edwardian era and is recognised for taking some of the earliest aerial photographs of London. Sitting beside Brewer in the rear of the car is Wilbur Wright. This is one of the last photographs of C.S. Rolls; he was tragically killed in a flying accident at Bournemouth in July 1910 when his Short-built Wright biplane broke up in the air.

George Clark of the Saxone Shoe Company in Kilmarnock was supplied with this 40/50hp, with coachwork by Dick Brothers, on 27 April 1912, through A. McGregor and Sons. Note the immaculate attire of the chauffeur, and (just visible) the small window in the top of the scuttle, immediately behind the AA badge. All Rolls-Royces were equipped with bespoke coachwork and Dick Brothers was one of a number of smaller enterprises specialising in individual commissions.

At the outbreak of the First World War the British Army clearly lacked motorised transport. Rolls-Royce, however, played a significant part in supplying the forces with a number of armoured vehicles including this 40/50hp light armoured car designed as a battery tender. At the wheel is T.E. Lawrence.

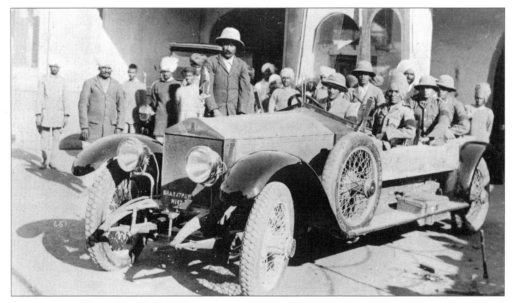

Working in hot dusty climates where extraordinary wear and tear could normally be expected, Rolls-Royces proved virtually failure proof. Often the vehicles were subjected to carrying unprecedented weight, and those destined for service in India and Afghanistan, for example, were mostly fitted with modified wheel bearings.

This fully armoured 40/50hp fitted out as a tank was built at the request of the Indian government for peace-keeping purposes and was designed and built by Vickers. Above the turret is the commander's cupola which, revolving independently, not only provided an observation point but reduced the risk of the operator getting a sniper's bullet through the head.

A 40/50hp, similar to that illustrated above, awaits delivery from Vickers' Erith works. Note, however, that there are certain differences between the two vehicles: the tank depicted here has camouflage and, instead of a single Vickers gun, there are two. T.E. Lawrence, the British soldier known as Lawrence of Arabia (1888–1935), said of the Rolls-Royce, 'A Rolls in the desert was "above rubies"'.

The engineering of Rolls-Royce cars made them exceptionally adept for work in the Middle and Far East. Pictured in the desert, this 40/50hp has been equipped with a wooden body along with a mounting for a Lewis gun which is clearly visible. Another interesting feature is the radiator cowling which, in this instance, has been opened to allow improved cooling. Note also the familiar shape of the radiator, together with the R-R monogram, behind the armour.

A number of Silver Ghosts and 40/50hp vehicles were destined for service in the desert, including this particular vehicle which has been loaded on to a Suez barge. Carrying a wooden body in the form of a pick-up truck, the car has not been fitted with any discernible armour; note, however, the twin rear wheels which would have provided additional traction and spread of weight over soft ground, and the rifle positioned at the side of the scuttle on the driver's right-hand side.

Not all Rolls-Royces were destined to provide luxury motoring, as can be judged by the foregoing illustrations of vehicles at work in the desert. This 40/50hp has been fitted with an ambulance body built by Rippon Bros of Huddersfield, Bradford and Leeds; the comfort of ride with a very able turn of speed would have made this ideal for such a purpose.

Even a Rolls-Royce cannot escape the ravages of war. Delivered to the Russian royal family, this Silver Ghost, originally a tourer with bodywork by Mann Egerton, was requisitioned by the Bolshevik government and used as personal transport by Lenin. The track conversion was carried out at the S.M. Kirov factory in Leningrad, and followed British crawler design of the period.

Henry Royce had a house built in the south of France at Le Canadel, where this picture was taken in 1913. The identity of the lady is not known but it is presumed to be either Minnie Royce or an acquaintance.

Henry Royce standing alongside a 40/50hp in 1921. One of the most successful of all Rolls-Royces, the 40/50's specification included a 6-cylinder side-valve engine with seven-bearing crankshaft, pressure lubrication and, until 1919, cast-iron pistons. After 1919 the pistons were manufactured using aluminium.

ROLLS-ROYCE BETWEEN THE WARS

The Hon. Francis Anson alongside his touring-bodied 40/50hp. The sheer size of the car is quite clear in this picture which shows, presumably, Anson taking part in either a hunt or shoot. Neither the location nor the event has been recorded but the attire has the suggestion of the twenties. From the background, which is only faintly visible, the hills are indicative of Scotland and may denote that the party is engaged on grouse shooting.

INTRODUCTION

The demand for cars in the post-war period was unprecedented and manufacturers throughout the motor industry fought to keep abreast with demand in order to supply an insatiable market. It was not only the popular makes which were affected; builders of luxury cars also had more orders than they could cope with, and as a result prices began to increase dramatically. As far as Rolls-Royce was concerned, a chassis costing a fraction under £1,000 before the war rose to almost £1,500, a figure which, in a very short period, escalated still further to over £2,000 by 1921.

The car with which Rolls-Royce spearheaded post-war production was the Twenty. Although nothing was lost in the way of quality and craftsmanship it was, nevertheless, a motor car designed to appeal to a whole new generation of discerning motorists. Introduced as an additional model to the 40/50, the Twenty broke entirely new ground: not only did it appear rather demure when viewed alongside the Edwardian Rolls-Royce, but its design and concept also raised a few eyebrows. This was the first Rolls-Royce to adopt a centrally positioned gear lever and handbrake, and the gearbox was also built in series with the engine. For Rolls-Royce, the rear axle was also novel in as much it was driven by an open propeller shaft and supported by semi-elliptic springs.

The Twenty's replacement was the 20/25 and although a development of the earlier model, the new car with its updated technology achieved the accolade of being the best-selling Rolls-Royce during the inter-war years. This in turn was superseded in 1936 by the 25/30, an altogether more modern machine which heralded not only the far greater use of proprietary components but also some rationalisation with the Bentley marque which had been acquired by Rolls-Royce in 1931.

There remained, of course, a specific demand for the luxury car that not even the Twenty and its successors could address. To meet such a requirement the Phantom I, a direct descendant of the Silver Ghost, was introduced in 1925; a more modern chassis design resulted in the appearance, in 1929, of the Phantom II, and the Phantom III, with its V12 engine, in 1935.

The most significant event in the history of the Rolls-Royce motor car during the period between the two world wars was the death, in April 1933, of Sir Henry Royce.

With Henry Royce at his drawing board is Ivan Evernden who joined Rolls-Royce in 1916. Evernden was responsible for some of the most respected cars in the world, and such was his commitment to the company that he designed his own headstone, which took the form of a Rolls-Royce radiator. He requested that, on his death, it be erected on his grave.

The Derby works c. 1922, clearly showing the production line occupied on producing the 40/50hp chassis. There is a ghostly atmosphere about the picture, which suggests that this was intended as a publicity photograph. The cleanliness and order of the factory is just what would be expected of Rolls-Royce and it is a wonder that the wheels, propped up against the pillar, were allowed to remain in that fashion.

A welcoming party for the Prince of Wales pictured some time between the Armistice and 1922, the celebrating crowd vigorously waving their Union Jacks. An open touring body was, at that time, deemed quite acceptable for public occasions and is in contrast to the present day when such vulnerability would be considered totally out of the question for state visits in terms of security.

The Derby works are pictured between 1922 and 1925, and show the 20hp under construction. Designed as a somewhat smaller car than its predecessors, Rolls-Royce recognised that the post-war motor car should be less expensive and that it should appeal to a wider market. The company did not, however, compromise on quality but did introduce a measure of simplification such as a central gear change (clearly visible on the car in the foreground) to control the 3-speed gearbox.

Royce started to design the 20hp chassis in 1920 with a series of prototype cars referred to as Goshawk. The third such car is depicted here with Henry Royce discussing the car's performance with A.G. Elliot, who was appointed chief engineer of the company in 1937. With Elliot is another engineer, Charles Jenner.

Built between 1922 and 1929, the 20hp, or Twenty as it is sometimes known, is, for many people, the epitome of the vintage Rolls-Royce. This 1924 car with 'Barker Barrel' coachwork is pictured during the late sixties, and appears to have been maintained beautifully. The 'barrel' expression is derived from the style of the coachwork which turns inwards towards the chassis side-member and whose shape provided an increased amount of interior accommodation.

When introduced, the Twenty was fitted with a central gear change position in the manner of most American cars of the period. This was not only in contrast to the 40/50hp models but to most other makes of car designed for the luxury market. In 1925 Rolls-Royce reverted to right-hand gear change where it remained for as long as the company produced vehicles with a manually operated gearbox, which was approximately the mid-fifties. In this picture, a Twenty, with Langra and Packer touring body and possibly fitted with a right-hand change lever, appears particularly resplendent.

The number of coachbuilders supplying bodies to Rolls-Royce was extensive and included some of the more famous companies such as Barker, Hooper, Salmons, Park Ward, Rippon and Cockshoot, to name but a few. A number of coachbuilders, such as Gurney Nutting and Freestone and Webb, did not start supplying Rolls-Royce until the twenties but were no less respected for that. This photograph, which appears to have been taken in more recent years, shows a diverse range of body styles associated with Rolls-Royce.

There can be few styles of coachwork more elegant than the Sedanca de Ville illustrated here with a Hooper-styled body. This Twenty has all the traditions of the carriage, even if it did mean the chauffeur was open to the elements.

The Rt Hon. David Lloyd George, prime minister from 1916 to 1922, poses for the photographer before stepping into his Phantom I. There does not appear to be any great significance about the package on the roof as cars were often fitted with a luggage grid. One suggestion is that Lloyd George may have borrowed a bread basket from a baker in which to secure his baggage.

Enthusiastic crowds have turned out to greet the Prince of Wales on his visit to the Isle of Wight on 22 July 1926. The car is a Phantom I which at the time was known as the New Phantom, and which was designed to meet demand for a larger and more modern car in the Rolls-Royce range. It was, nevertheless, a development of the 40/50hp chassis but with a new overhead valve engine of 7.6 litres. Introduced in 1925, the Phantom I continued to be built until 1929.

The rakish design of this tourer together with its white wall tyres suggests that it is not what an established British coachbuilder might have produced. The real clue as to the car's identity lies of course with the Illinois registration plate; not a British Rolls-Royce but an American specimen with Brewster Ascot bodywork. Brewster produced its first coachwork for Rolls-Royce in 1908 when a landaulette body was mounted on a Silver Ghost chassis; in 1914 the company became a Rolls-Royce agent and, in 1925, was taken over by Rolls-Royce of America Inc. During the Second World War, Brewster turned to aircraft production and is chiefly remembered for the barrel-like 'Buffalo' fighter.

Henry Royce appears to be pleased with the performance of the prototype New Phantom which has been fitted with an open touring body by Hooper. The photograph, which is signed by Royce and dated 1925, was taken at West Wittering, Royce's home on the south coast in Sussex. The car was a particular favourite of Royce, who used it extensively as his personal car. Originally given the project name of Seagull, the new Phantom's development was undertaken in strict secrecy, a point made by Ian Rimmer in his book on Rolls-Royce and Bentley experimental cars.

There can hardly be a Rolls-Royce (or any other car) with a more opulent interior than this Phantom I supplied to C.W. Gasque in 1927. A collector of antique French furniture, the customer ordered that his car, which had coachwork built by Clark of Wolverhampton, be appointed in the style of Louis XIV with Aubusson needlework upholstery. The present whereabouts of the car is unknown but for many years it remained in the collection of the late Stanley Sears, a devoted Rolls-Royce enthusiast and recognised authority on the marque.

In 1925, Royce decided that a Sports Phantom should be built to demonstrate the Phantom's performance potential given a suitably designed body. Fitted with an open sports body supplied by Barker, the car, an experimental vehicle built on chassis 10EX, underwent a series of trials under the care of W.A. Robotham and in this picture he can be seen alongside the car, having made a number of test runs at Brooklands between 1926 and 1927. It was at Brooklands that a maximum lap speed of over 91mph was recorded; no doubt the wings of the car had been removed in order to lighten the weight and reduce the drag coefficient.

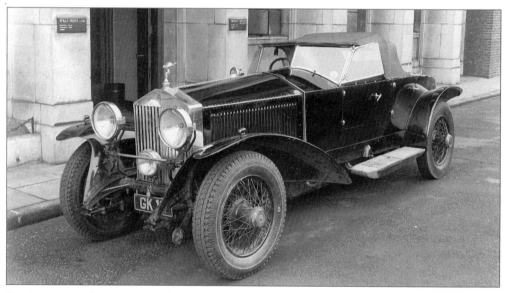

Standing outside the entrance to the Derby factory, this exquisite sports tourer started life as a Sports Phantom experimental car, the second of three such vehicles to have been built. Bearing the registration number CH 7234, the car, in chassis form, began trials in January 1928 and it was not until the following month that the streamlined Barker body was fitted. As an experimental car (chassis no. 16EX), the testing of this vehicle was curtailed after only 430 miles when it was sent to the sales department at Lillie Hall where it was re-registered GK 12. Befitting its elegance, the coachwork was finished in Curzon blue and polished aluminium.

This delightful study in early motoring may have been taken in Switzerland. The car, a Phantom I, is deep in mountainous isolation, and it is interesting to see the state of the road surface. The Phantoms were designed for reliability and comfort over long distances and were, therefore, ideal for touring in the grand style. Nevertheless, to cope with these conditions, the driver would have required the utmost skill and knowledge.

A careful inspection of this photograph will reveal that the car is fitted with left-hand drive. In fact it is the first LH drive Rolls-Royce, an experimental car fitted with a Barker sports saloon body. The photograph was taken in France around 1929/30 with Henry Royce, E.W. Hives (later Lord Hives) and A.G. Elliot. Also in the picture is Nurse Ethel Aubin who, for twenty years, cared for Henry Royce and was in close but unobtrusive attendance throughout his long period of poor health. Used as a test vehicle, this car was the first Rolls-Royce to be tested at the Montlhéry race track near Paris; following exhaustive trials the Barker sports body was replaced with a Fernandez Sedanca de Ville body and the car sold to a French customer. It is believed the vehicle has survived and was last recorded as being in the Paris area.

In 1931 Henry Royce was made a baronet but even as Sir Frederick Henry Royce he preferred to be known as Henry Royce, mechanic. Although mostly a calm and gentle character, Royce, especially in his younger years, could be known to bark in an almost terrifying manner. A burly countryman who was happier dressed in sloppy tweeds and boots, he often displayed a kindly and generous personality which was never more in evidence than when, on an occasion when he kept his team of mechanics working day and night, he took them, complete with oily clothes, to his home at 3 a.m. for refreshments. Following a severe illness and operation in 1912, Royce suffered poor health for over twenty years. He died at home, at Elmstead, West Wittering, Sussex, on 22 April 1933.

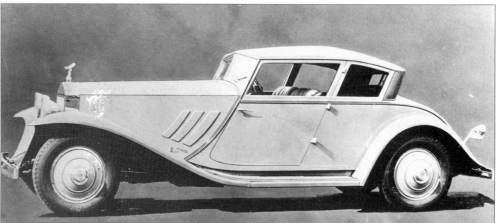

Some enthusiasts might consider the styling of this American Phantom I totally outrageous; others, however, would rather appreciate the car's extravagant if not completely eccentric coachwork. Whatever one's view, the radical appearance of this very special Rolls-Royce successfully stopped the New York Motor Show in its tracks when it was unveiled in 1930; given the name Windblown coupé by William Brewster, the super sports coupé was somewhat unpractical in as much as its seats were positioned so low that the driver almost sat on the floor and the headroom was minimal. Not surprisingly, the car's existence was kept a closely guarded secret until the opening of the show.

Instead of the Spirit of Ecstasy, Lord Baden-Powell's car carries the standard of the Scout movement on the radiator housing. The car, which Baden-Powell affectionately referred to as the 'jam roll' and which was presented to him by the Scout movement, became a frequent and respected visitor at scouting events.

Priced at £3,000, this elegant Rolls-Royce was the most expensive vehicle on display at the 1931 London Motor Show. With dust sheets still surrounding the car, the young lady is obviously intrigued at the unashamed luxury and craftsmanship. A close look at the Spirit of Ecstasy will reveal that the mascot is turned through 90°.

Sir Malcolm Campbell (1885–1948) at Brooklands alongside an H.J. Mulliner Phantom II Continental (chassis no. 55GX). Sir Malcolm, himself an enthusiastic Rolls-Royce owner, was at one time holder of both land and water speed records and was often called upon to conduct trials of cars, usually for such journals as *Field* and *Country Life*. The registration plate is of some significance: the GO prefix with similarly low suffix numbers was used by the Talbot racing team on their cars during the same period. Note the array of auxiliary lamps and klaxons on the front of the car, and the driving lamp attached to the front offside door pillar.

The 20/25, a development of the Twenty, was Rolls-Royce's best-selling car during the inter-war years. It shared certain characteristics with the Phantom II in that the chassis configuration was very similar, but differed from the earlier Twenty models by having a taller radiator and vertical shutters. The shutters on later Twenty cars, incidentally, were also of the vertical type. Mechanically, the car incorporated several improvements over the model it replaced; the brakes were more effective and the engine balance allowed it to run faster. The car pictured here is an early tourer; note the rear screens which allowed added protection from the elements to passengers sitting at the back of the car.

Few Rolls-Royces could have claim to a more sporting design of coachwork than this 1931 20/25 (chassis no. GFT43). Produced by Corsica, the 20/25 was originally supplied to the Marquis of Cholmondeley and is unusual in its styling treatment which, even by 1931 standards, is remarkably adventurous. Note the two small rear windows, sloping back, and unusual wings. From the shape of the bodywork a split windscreen instead of the one-piece affair would not have looked out of place.

Photographed at the Last Drop village inn, near Bolton, in Lancashire, this 1932 20/25 tourer gives the already charming scene added character. Pictured during the seventies – the trouser flares give a good indication of the era – the Gill-Alexandra-bodied car looks resplendent and would have been representative of one of the later coachbuilt bodies to have been delivered from this relatively small London coachbuilder. Coachbuilding before the First World War, T.H. Gill & Co. ceased production at their Paddington premises in 1935.

HRH King George V's visit to RAF Hendon was recorded by the camera in 1935. His majesty is wearing the uniform of Marshal of the Royal Air Force and is accompanied by his two sons, Edward, Prince of Wales, and Albert, Duke of York. The cars in the foreground are all Phantom IIs, a model that was introduced in 1929 and which remained in production until 1935, some 1,767 chassis having been built. Hendon, a most important airfield and one of the most famous, is now home to the Royal Air Force Museum.

This is something of a mystery photograph; what appears to be either a 20/25 or Phantom II which has undergone radical and extensive surgery in order to transform the vehicle into a half-cab pick-up truck which is being run on trade plates. For what purpose the conversion was made is also unclear but the equipment positioned on the nearside aft of the cab could possibly be for fire-fighting. The location is also of interest; note the Ford V8 Pilot parked behind the Rolls-Royce, the left-hand drive jeep together with an odd assortment of vehicles scattered around the factory yard. First impressions suggest the Derby factory although, in fact, it could be anywhere.

Pictured in Afghanistan, this Phantom II appears to be making relatively light work of the desert conditions, the full load and hostile environment having little or no apparent effect on the car's performance. As can be seen the Phantom II was an extremely handsome motor car, the length of the bonnet together with the radiator positioned aft of the front axle providing for a particular elegance. Having been introduced in 1929, the Phantom II's chassis was, in effect, an enlarged Twenty and incorporated many of that car's features, such as the gearbox built in unit with the engine and open propeller shaft. Developments of the Phantom II chassis included the provision of thermostatically operated radiator shutters and improved chassis lubrication.

There is a distinct elegance about this Barker-bodied Airflow saloon built on a Phantom III chassis. When introduced in 1935, some serious attention was given to streamlining, and instead of upright body styles a general smoothing out of wing lines and raking of windscreens was becoming fashionable. In the best of taste, the Airflow has adapted to the changes in style very successfully and is worthy of its 'sports saloon' designation.

France was an appropriate testing venue for experimental cars, especially when collecting experience aimed towards continental motoring. Châteauroux was a particularly popular place, not only because of its central position, but also because a number of major roads radiate in all directions, connecting with different regions of the country. An experimental Phantom II, which was designed with the American market in mind, is pictured here outside an hotel, possibly near the Swiss border. Conducting the trials are three Rolls-Royce personnel, Eric Platford, W. Robotham and John Maddox.

This Phantom is pictured outside an hotel, possibly in France. Note the tram-lines and the car behind the Rolls-Royce, which is either a 4-cylinder (C4) or 6-cylinder (C6) Citroën. The Phantom II models were initially introduced to compete against such cars as the Bentley, as well as other prestigious sporting saloons of the period, and the theme was continued with the Phantom III which was equipped with a V12 engine.

One of the most unusual coachwork designs to adorn a Rolls-Royce chassis (chassis no. 3AX79), this H.J. Mulliner saloon was built for Alan Butler of de Havilland Aircraft and once owned by Viscount Montgomery of Alamein. Apart from the enclosed rear wheel-arches and the massive proportions of the rear styling, note the distinctive roof line with the inverted split windscreen and oddly shaped front pillars. Between the wars, H.J. Mulliner was, perhaps, best known for its characteristic saloons which perpetuated razor-edge styling with thin windscreen pillars which, at that time, was considered particularly elegant.

This rather severe and staid Phantom was built for the Viceroy of India. The styling is typical of that usually adopted for official cars and whatever opinion one has of the lack of any streamlining it is, nevertheless, beautifully designed and appointed. Note the radiator, the massive headlamps and the klaxons, which are most impressive.

The late Stanley Sears amassed a most important, and enviable, collection of Rolls-Royces, three of which are seen here. Nearest the camera is the Phantom I Sedanca de Ville with its interior finished in the style of Louis XIV; note the exquisite appointment together with the striking paint finish. In the middle is a Phantom II, again with Sedanca-type coachwork. Furthest from the camera is a Phantom III and the sheer impressiveness of this car can be gauged from the size of the other vehicles.

As well as a factory in Derby, Rolls-Royce also had a London service centre where these cars are pictured. With their majestic radiators, each bearing the Spirit of Ecstasy, few cars could possibly match the mystique, quality and good taste that Rolls-Royce could offer. It was at the London Service Centre at Hythe Road, Willesden, where owners of Rolls-Royce cars could attend a school of instruction – which is still available at Crewe to this day – to derive not only the best possible service from their cars, but how to treat them with the respect they deserved.

In what appears to be a publicity photograph taken in a quintessentially English setting, possibly in Derbyshire or the Lake District, this 25/30hp Wraith makes a most handsome sight. With styling typical of the late thirties and sporting a degree of streamlining, the Wraith was designed as a companion model to the Phantom III and incorporated such refinements as independent front suspension and a light alloy engine. It was also designed as a more sophisticated counterpart to the Bentley.

The complete absence of any activity again suggests a publicity photograph. This is the Derby factory around 1937–8. As well as a Rolls-Royce 25/30 in the course of construction in the foreground, the production line includes a number of 4¼ Bentley models. The subject of Bentley is to be covered in the next chapter but it is pertinent to explain that in 1931 the firm was acquired by Rolls-Royce and production of Bentley cars was transferred from London to Derby. The 25/30 Rolls-Royce was introduced in 1936 and the basic design of the 4¼ litre engine was shared with the Bentley.

The activity at the Derby works in 1937 surrounds a visit by the lord mayor. From the crowd that has gathered at the factory gates there is obviously an air of excitement, especially as the cars are starting to leave. The cars in production at Derby at the time would have been the 25/30, Bentley 4¼-litre and Phantom III; the engines of the 25/30 and the Bentley were similar but the latter used different carburettors and had a higher compression. The Phantom III was fitted with a 7.3 litre V12 engine and was designed to meet growing competition from manufacturers of other large and powerful cars. The design of the V12 was, in fact, Sir Henry Royce's swan-song; it was his final contribution to the cars bearing his name and sadly his design team was unable to complete the engine before his death. The second part of the thirties was a period when Rolls-Royce was considering rationalising chassis design, and it was work carried out in the immediate pre-war years which set the standard for post-war car production.

This Wraith is pictured in Glencoe and appears almost out of place among the rugged and dramatic scenery. The appointment of the Wraith, as can be imagined, was luxurious and certainly ideal for a sophisticated touring holiday in Scotland. Produced between 1938 and 1939, some 491 Wraith chassis were built.

This James Young six-light saloon built on the Wraith chassis has a superb style which is clean and very unfussy. The location appears to be a favourite one for the coachbuilder, as many of the company's publicity photographs were taken in a similar position. One of the most respected of all coachbuilders, the Bromley firm was acquired by Jack Barclay, the famous Rolls-Royce dealership, in 1937. The coachbuilder switched to war work in 1939 and the coachbuilding premises were badly damaged by bombing.

The Second World War saw the establishment of the Home Guard which, following the successful television series, is now better known as Dad's Army! In this evocative picture, members of the Home Guard proudly pose for the photographer with a 40/50hp Rolls-Royce which has been converted for use as a breakdown truck. The vehicle is the property of Moore's of Brighton, motor engineers of Russell Square, and presumably has been pressed into service with the Brighton Home Guard battalion who appear to be dressed ready for action. Note the highly polished bell on the cab roof of the vehicle, and the auxiliary lamps on the scuttle.

THE BENTLEY TRADITION

A gathering of Bentley enthusiasts is always an auspicious occasion and none more than that depicted in this photograph. Owners of such cars as these are usually more than happy to enter their vehicles for competitive events and to enjoy the spirit in which these cars were intended. W.O. Bentley would no doubt have been honoured to know that cars bearing his name are still revered to such an extent.

INTRODUCTION

Established in 1919 by W.O. Bentley, the marque bearing its founder's name is revered throughout the world to the extent that there can be few devotees of the motor car who do not experience some twinge of nostalgia, and a degree of British pride, at seeing the famous winged-B mascot. The mere mention of the car conjures up stirring thoughts of Brooklands, Montlhéry and Le Mans, rekindling memories of the golden age of motor sport glorified by a daring brigade of racing drivers that included Tim Birkin and the Bentley Boys. Sitting behind the wheel of a vintage Bentley, considered by many the epitome of the British sports car, with helmet and goggles and looking over that impressive bonnet while listening to the growling exhaust is, for most, but a dream.

The first car to bear the Bentley name was conceived in an office on the top floor of a building in Conduit Street, close to the Rolls-Royce showrooms, but it was at a mews garage just off London's Baker Street that the prototype car was built. Although the fledgling company had a polished chassis to display at the London Motor Show at Olympia in November that year, it was not until January 1920 that the first complete car was tested and acclaimed by Sammy Davis of *The Autocar*, who himself was later to become one of the legendary Bentley Boys.

While the prototype Bentley was being built, thought was being given to the establishment of a factory. W.O. heard of some land that was for sale at Cricklewood in north-west London and it was there, adjacent to the North Circular Road, that a brick-built test shop was erected during the early months of 1920. From those modest beginnings the premises had, within ten years, expanded considerably, a feat made possible only by the intervention of Woolf Barnato, the racing driver millionaire, who invested heavily in the company.

The Cricklewood cars of the twenties, the 3 litre, 6 litre and Speed Six, the 4½ litre and mighty 8 litre, were among the finest anywhere in the world, but that did not prevent Bentley Motors Ltd suffering severe financial difficulties in 1931. A receiver was appointed, and it was anticipated that Napier, wishing to return to car production, would acquire Bentley; in the event, it was Rolls-Royce who outbid them. As Bentley Motors (1931) Ltd, production of cars was transferred from Cricklewood to Derby and, in 1933, the first new model, the 3½ litre, was announced. Although the Bentley marque lost much of its identity during the sixties and seventies, this, happily, has now been substantially restored.

Walter Owen Bentley was born in London on 16 September 1888, the youngest of nine children. W.O., as he became universally known, was sixteen before he rode in a motor car and, in his autobiography, he admits to having more interest in the steam locomotive in his early years than any other form of transportation. Bentley's love of railways led him to serve an apprenticeship with the Great Northern Railway at Doncaster from 1904 but he soon came to realise that this was not the industry in which he wanted to make his career.

While at Doncaster, W.O. had discovered the motorcycle; on leave in London, he visited a cycle shop and came away with a 3hp Quadrant which was at least third- or fourth-hand. It was this machine which introduced the young W.O. to competition events and to getting more out of an engine than would normally have been expected. It was on a motorcycle, a Rex, that W.O. was introduced to Brooklands while taking part in the One-Hour event in 1909, two years or so after the circuit had been opened.

Bentley's spell of duty with the National Cab Company, and the fleet of Unic taxicabs it operated, was responsible for creating a lure for four wheels instead of two, and it wasn't long before the young W.O. bought his first motor car, a Riley. Events brought the motor car even closer to W.O.'s heart when he joined his brother in selling the DFP car for a firm which had the franchise for several other French cars. It was this relationship which eventually led Bentley to form his own company, Bentley Motors Ltd, in 1919.

Although W.O. Bentley established his company in 1919 and exhibited a polished chassis at Olympia, the first prototype car was not ready until 1920. It was, however, another two years before the first customers could take delivery of their cars. This photograph, taken at Le Mans in 1924, shows W.O. standing between chief tester Frank Clement and John Duff, drivers of the latter's 3-litre Bentley. The event, which was considered an ideal showcase in which to give the car a good airing and further its publicity, proved to be an ordeal for both the vehicle and its drivers, for not only was the night section undertaken with just one headlamp (the other had been broken by a stone) but the fuel tank was pierced by another flying stone the following day. Frank Clement had to return to the pit to collect some fuel and set off on a bicycle with two cans slung around his neck! In spite of such setbacks, the car finished a creditable fourth! Almost hidden in the pits can be seen A.F.C. Hillstead who ran the sales department throughout the life of the old company, and was author of that most evocative Bentley history, *Those Bentley Days*.

Unlike most Rolls-Royce cars, Bentleys were recognised for their racing prowess, well illustrated in this photograph of Eddie Hall at the wheel of his own 4¼-litre car. He was no stranger to motor racing or Bentleys and was well known at Brooklands. A.F. Rivers Fletcher, ex-Bentley apprentice and life-long authority on the marque, recalls Hall at speed at Brooklands in the early thirties, where he would often be seen flying through the air after hitting the notorious bump on the track's outer circuit over the River Wey! This is an evocative photograph and is full of action as he hurls the big car through a bend while competing in the 1936 TT Race; note the enthusiastic crowd of spectators, as well as the banner advertising *The Autocar* which, at that time, cost a mere 4*d*.

Another picture of Eddie Hall with his 4¼-litre Bentley taken on the same occasion. Eddie's performances at Brooklands during the thirties managed to evoke memories of what, for many Bentley enthusiasts, was considered the golden era of motor racing when such personalities as Woolf Barnato, Tim Birkin, Dr J.D. Benjafield, Sammy Davis, Dudley Froy and others dominated the scene. The sheer skill of racing a car such as the Bentley is shown to good effect here and Hall can be seen putting as much effort as possible into pushing the car into the bend.

Few cars could claim such elegance as this Foursome Coupé de Ville dating from around 1934. The Derby Bentleys, so named as to distinguish them from the Cricklewood cars, are now among the most sought after of both marques. Despite some initial opposition from the purists, the Derby Bentleys soon found enthusiastic customers which considered these to be every bit as good as the models of earlier years.

In this scene at the London Service Centre, a 4¼-litre Bentley is undergoing maintenance. The rear wheels have been removed, possibly for overhaul of the brakes. Next to it appears to be a Rolls-Royce 20/25; with its body removed, the extent of the work is obviously much greater than what would be considered 'routine' and the question to be asked is whether the vehicle is undergoing accident repair. As for the workshop, note its orderly state and tidiness.

Following the transfer of car production from Cricklewood to Derby there was a gradual move by Rolls-Royce towards a rationalisation policy whereby the number of chassis designs was not only limited but shared between different models. The architect of this policy was W.A. Robotham who sensed that changes in the motor industry were such that, were Rolls-Royce to continue as it had in the past, the future would indeed be bleak. Robotham also recognised, from developments in the American car industry, that the days of coachbuilt cars were numbered and there existed a need to adopt production methods that, at the time, appeared extremely radical. The car that was seen to lead Robotham's directive was the Bentley Mk V which, designed as a 1940 model, made its appearance in 1939. Production of this particular Bentley was curtailed after only eleven cars had been built due to the onset of war and did not continue when vehicle manufacturing resumed in 1946. Pictured at the Derby works, this Mk V chassis shows the car's independent front suspension and the engine which it shared with the Rolls-Royce Wraith, but with twin SU carburettors.

The Bentley Mk V, as introduced in 1939; this, the last of the Derby Bentleys, was designed around a rationalised chassis range which was introduced mainly as a cost-cutting exercise. The Mk V depicted here has coachwork by Park Ward, and is clearly a very elegant car. When post-war car building resumed, not at Derby but at Crewe, production of the Mk V was not included. The fact that only eleven Mk Vs were built has added to the car's value, not only in terms of price but in Rolls-Royce and Bentley history too.

At the same time as the Mk V Bentley was introduced, work was well under way with a radically designed car known as the Corniche, which had coachwork by Van Vooren of Paris. Using a modified version of the Mk V's chassis, the Corniche, possibly the most famous of all experimental Bentleys, was jointly designed by Ivan Evernden and Georges Paulin, and is shown here displaying its unique styling, which incorporated the latest ideas in streamlining. As well as the split windscreen and the concealed rear wheel-arches, note the car's frontal treatment which lacks the traditional Bentley radiator. It has been claimed that this particular styling feature was only a temporary measure designed to disguise the fact, for testing purposes, that it was a Bentley. The car encompassed several interesting design features, not least of which were those intended to reduce the vehicle's overall weight, which amounted to a little over 34cwt. There is a distinct elegance about this car which is accentuated by the front wing line, the side lamps and the shape of the headlamps. The 'Cyclops' lamp is also a feature which was found on a number of post-war models, both British and American, and included the Rover P4 and Austin Atlantic as well as the Studebaker and Tucker.

This photograph was taken while the car was undergoing trials on the continent shortly before the outbreak of war in 1939 and, sadly, the car was severely damaged in a road accident. The body was removed from the chassis, which was returned to Derby, and the body sent for repair at a coachbuilder in Châteauroux; when repaired, the body was en route to England but did not survive a bombing raid on Dieppe while waiting to be shipped across the Channel.

Georges Paulin, incidentally, was shot by the Germans when France was occupied; letters and drawings pertaining to Rolls-Royce were found in his office in Paris and he was treated as a collaborator.

Possibly the most evocative of all Bentleys is this racing machine known as the 'Embericos Bentley' which, it is said, was built for the famous Greek racing driver. Inspired by Walter Sleator, Paris dealer for Rolls-Royce, this was the fastest of all pre-war Bentleys and, when driven at Brooklands in 1939 with George Eyston at the wheel, it achieved over 114mph. The car was the subject of a detailed report in *The Autocar* of February 1939 following tests that encompassed both the French Routes Nationales and the German Autobahn. So favourable was the account that the feature's headline simply read 'Touring at 100mph!'

This is no ordinary Bentley but an experimental car, with coachwork by Park Ward, designed to further the performance of the Mk V. Known officially as the Comet but unofficially within the company as the 'Scalded Cat', due to its blistering performance, the aim of the car was to boost the Mk V's top speed to 100mph, which it did using an 8-cylinder B80 engine. The body was aluminium panelled on a wood frame, and at 36cwt the grey-painted car was relatively light for its size. 'Scalded Cat' was loaned to a number of special customers, including HRH Prince Philip, the Duke of Edinburgh, who was so impressed with its performance that he was rather reluctant to return the car to Rolls-Royce.

CREWE: A NEW ERA

This evocative picture, dating from the late forties, shows Bentley Mk VI cars in the finishing (or 16) shop prior to handing over to the car bond as finished cars. The care and attention to detail, never relaxed at Rolls-Royce, is evident; notice the gleaming chrome and polished paintwork, even the tin of polish on the floor. At this stage in the build process the cars are still minus their wheel discs and radiator mascots. In June 1947, a Mk VI similar to that depicted here cost over £3,300 inclusive of purchase tax; a Daimler saloon could be purchased for a little under half the price while a small popular car, such as an Austin, Morris or Ford, cost around a tenth.

INTRODUCTION

When car manufacturing resumed after the war it was not the Derby factory on which Rolls-Royce centred production, but Crewe, in a factory which, under the 'shadow factory' arrangement, had been designed for building aero-engines as part of the war effort. It was there, at Pyms Lane on what had once been Merrill's Farm, that the famous Merlins which powered the RAF's fighters and bombers were produced. While Rolls-Royce continued to develop engines for both military and commercial aircraft at Derby, they found they had the capacity, together with a skilled workforce at Crewe, to which car production could be entrusted.

W.A. Robotham's rationalisation policies, conceived pre-war, were adopted and, because many of the specialist coachbuilders did not resume business after the war years, an element of standardisation was also fostered. This meant that while some bespoke coachbuilding applications remained in the production of post-war models, the greater number of cars were, for Rolls-Royce, manufactured using wholly new techniques which included the buying-in of Standard Steel bodies made by Pressed Steel at Cowley, Oxford.

Perhaps better known for body shells fitted to some of the more popular makes of car, the Pressed Steel bodies were built to Rolls-Royce's specifications, Ivan Evernden and John Blatchley having been responsible for the styling.

The first of the post-war cars to be produced at Crewe was, ironically, not a Rolls-Royce at all but a Bentley, the Mk VI. Although announced in spring 1946, difficulties caused by a shortage of raw materials and components prevented production from getting under way until the autumn; deliveries, therefore, were delayed until the end of the year. Despite the fact that a certain number of die-hard enthusiasts were reluctant to accept it as a 'proper' Rolls-Royce product, the car was, widely acclaimed.

A Rolls-Royce with a Standard Steel body, the Silver Dawn, did not appear until 1949. It was pre-dated by the Silver Wraith which was constructed more in the traditional Rolls-Royce manner with its chassis designed to accommodate custom-built coachwork. As the economic climate improved, Rolls-Royce was able to increase production and offer models, such as the R-Type Bentley, the Continental and a modified Silver Dawn. These, and their coachbuilt variants, built by such famous companies as James Young, Park Ward and H.J. Mulliner, many of which have survived, enjoy a particular place in the history of the Rolls-Royce motor car and are highly revered.

Conduit Street, the London home of Rolls-Royce since the early days of the company and before the untimely death of C.S. Rolls. In this photograph, which was taken in 1957, some of the post-war models can be seen through the showroom windows. Look at the gentleman donning his hat as he leaves the premises – has he just placed an order for a new car? The picture is evocative of 1950s London; turning the corner is a London taxicab, an Austin FX3, and parked is another Austin, possibly an A70 Hereford. Just visible behind the taxi is either a Rolls-Royce Silver Cloud or Bentley S-Series.

Pictured in the Crewe factory, one of the first cars to leave the assembly line is ready to be delivered. This is the 'there and back' chassis line at the south end of main shop, with the stores in the background; the other row of bodies is in the 'north-bound lane', which did a 180° turn at the far end to arrive here as finished cars. Post-war production began in 1946 amidst dire shortages of raw materials and components and although manufacturing had been intended to begin in the spring of that year, it was autumn before scenes such as this were witnessed. The car in the foreground is a Bentley Mk VI, the model which introduced post-war car building at Crewe. In the background work is under way preparing partly finished vehicles and on the right can be seen a line of Bentleys at various stages of manufacture.

This is something of a mystery photograph, as the car, with obvious similarities to the Bentley Mk VI, has certain styling aspects not seen on the production vehicle. Note the large headlamps, larger section front wings and the side-mounted wheel carrier; a closer look at the bonnet will reveal that it is longer than that usually found on the Standard Steel saloon. The car is, in fact, an experimental vehicle, the second 'Scalded Cat', which was built on the production line at Crewe. A Pressed Steel body was utilised but a longer bonnet concealed a straight 8-cylinder engine instead of the 6-cylinder fitted to the Mk VI. The maximum speed recorded for this car was 96mph, although it has to be mentioned that fuel starvation problems prevented a higher speed being attained. The 8-cylinder engine was eventually changed for a 6-cylinder unit and the car continued in service until at least 1956, by which time well over 100,000 miles had been recorded.

The car's registration (Cheshire being the licensing authority) dates from 1948 but the location of the photograph is uncertain. A later picture of the car (not shown in this book) reveals that the headlamps have been replaced with types more akin to those fitted to the Bentley Mk VI.

As well as Crewe, Rolls-Royce also maintained their London coachbuilding premises under the auspices of Park Ward. It is at Park Ward that this very elegant convertible, built on the Mk VI Bentley chassis, is given a final inspection before being made ready for delivery. Viewed against a Standard Steel saloon, this Park Ward car shows a number of variations apart from the bodywork. Note that the doors are front-hinged and that the wings are longer than those found on the Crewe cars; the hood is also power-operated. A model similar to this was ordered by the King of Denmark.

In 1949, Rolls-Royce introduced the Silver Dawn which, like the Bentley Mk VI, was designed to accommodate a standardised Pressed Steel body. Pictured at Crewe, it will be noticed that only the offside headlamp has been fitted, and the bonnet has yet to be installed, as has much of the trim.

Post-war production of Rolls-Royce cars did not get under way until 1947, when the Silver Wraith was introduced. It was usual when road testing a chassis to fit a test rig body which was specially designed to accentuate any detectable chassis noise. Once back at the factory, any rectification work found necessary was completed. Test rig bodies were used until Rolls-Royce implemented those models designed with an integral chassis and body.

This imposing view of a Silver Dawn was taken outside the main entrance to the Crewe factory. The model was introduced in 1949 expressly to satisfy the export market and differed from the Bentley Mk VI in a number of ways. Silver Dawns were fitted with twin fog-lamps and heavier bumpers and were mechanically similar apart from the engine, which was the same as that used for the Silver Wraith with only a single carburettor. The interior of the Silver Dawn was identical to that of the Bentley except for the arrangement of the facia, which had separate gauges grouped around a central speedometer. Right-hand drive cars were fitted with a right-hand gear change but left-hand drive models employed a column gear lever.

In this 1951 scene at Conduit Street, the London showrooms of Rolls-Royce, can be seen, nearest to the camera, a Bentley Mk VI two-door saloon with coachwork by Park Ward. To the right and in the background, is another Bentley, a Standard Steel saloon. The Park Ward car is fitted with left-hand steering while that of the Standard Steel car is on the right. Nearest the window, however, is a majestic Silver Wraith with coachwork by H.J. Mulliner and built as a Sedanca de Ville: it will be noted that this has left-hand drive. Outside the showrooms can be seen a Bentley Mk VI, which is possibly a company demonstrator.

Before the advent of Rolls-Royce's rationalisation policy, all cars were fitted with the traditional custom-built body. The Standard Steel saloons, with their Pressed Steel bodies, found a ready market, especially as there was no compromise in quality. The only criticism concerned that of the quality of steel, which was in no way a reflection of either Pressed Steel or Rolls-Royce, but a consequence of the period of austerity following the war. To avert any criticism, however, the number of early production cars that have survived is impressive, especially when compared with models of other post-war cars. The Silver Dawn was notably appreciated in America where the Bentley marque never achieved the same prestige.

The Rolls-Royce Silver Wraith (nearest the camera) and the Bentley Mk VI make a handsome pair of motor cars. Unlike the Mk VI, which was designed to accommodate either a Standard Steel or coachbuilt body, the Silver Wraith was produced as a chassis only on which custom bodies could be fitted. For the customer, there was a choice of several bespoke coachbuilders, including Park Ward, H.J. Mulliner, James Young, Hooper and Freestone & Webb. The Silver Wraith's chassis was one of two rationalised designs introduced after the war and was similar to that utilised for the Bentley Mk VI and Rolls-Royce Silver Dawn, except that it was some 7 inches longer in short-wheelbase form.

Seen at the 1952 London Motor Show, this Silver Wraith four-door saloon is particularly elegant. The coachwork has all the hallmarks of Rippon, the Huddersfield coachbuilder, who exhibited almost identical cars at the 1950 and 1951 shows and who, in total, built five bodies for the Silver Wraith chassis. As would be expected from such an old-established and well-respected firm, the appointment of these cars was in the finest taste.

The Silver Dawn was not available for home market sales until 1952, all previous cars having been destined for export to earn much-needed revenue for the exchequer. This right-hand drive makes an elegant picture, especially with the Bentley, an early example of the T-Series, in the background. ZO is a Dublin registration and dates from February 1952 to May 1953. The occasion appears to be a gathering of the Rolls-Royce Enthusiasts' Club at Charterhouse.

This Bentley Mk VI clearly demonstrates the car's handsome styling which was penned by Ivan Evernden and John Blatchley, the latter having been recruited to Rolls-Royce from Gurney Nutting, the highly respected coachbuilding firm. The car displays a degree of razor-edge styling, which was very popular before and immediately after the war. The fine appointment of the interior can be clearly seen and it is worth noting the doors, which are rear-hinged and universally known as the 'suicide' type, an arrangement which was very convenient for entry and exit, and a feature of many cars up to the mid-fifties.

The Bentley was the car often specified by professional people, such as lawyers and surgeons. It was also frequently the choice, along with cars such as the Silver Wraith, of the aristocracy, but this Mk VI does appear somewhat incongruous in this isolated setting with little but mountain sheep to add to the scenery. Presumably the barn is where the car is kept! The car in question is carrying a Cheshire registration dating from 1951, probably the year the car was supplied.

At the London Motor Show in 1952, Rolls-Royce exhibited four cars on its stand. Nearest the camera is a Silver Wraith six-light saloon while behind it, nearest to the technicians in white coats, is a Silver Dawn with Pressed Steel body. Opposite is a Silver Wraith enclosed limousine (nearest the camera) and a Silver Wraith touring limousine. On the Bentley stand, furthest from the camera, is the R-Type, successor to the Mk VI, with Pressed Steel bodywork. The R-Type could be easily distinguished from the Mk VI by the extended boot and longer rear wing line, the same modifications being made to Silver Dawn cars. To its right can be seen the magnificent lines of the Bentley R-Type Continental and, nearest the camera, a Park Ward 2-door convertible, ahead of which is a Park Ward 2-door saloon.

Park Ward, Rolls-Royce's in-house coachbuilder, displayed this majestic Silver Wraith long-wheelbase touring saloon at the 1953 London Motor Show. As would be expected of these fine cars – of which over sixty were built – they were beautifully appointed.

This is the Rolls-Royce and Bentley stand at the 1953 Geneva Motor Show. Nearest the camera is a Graber-bodied Bentley Continental, one of only three such cars to have been built, and, to the left, is an H.J. Mulliner R-Type Continental. Behind the Graber-bodied car can be seen a Silver Dawn.

The winter sunshine together with the lingering frost gives this picture of a Silver Wraith seven-passenger limousine a sharp and invigorating feel. The fact that the car is equipped with left-hand drive indicates that it was designed for use abroad on diplomatic business. The coachwork, by Hooper, is rather formal and very different to the designs the coachbuilder would have used for its touring limousines. Several cars were prepared to a similar design, all being intended for use by her majesty's ambassadors.

From a distance the Bentley R-Type saloon is almost indistinguishable from its predecessor, the Mk VI. The most obvious identifying feature is the styling of the boot, which, on the R-Type cars, is somewhat extended. The modification gave the car a more athletic look which was only made possible by virtue of the fact that the restyling affected the car from the central pillar rearward. A careful study between this and a Mk VI will also reveal a lower rear wheel-arch and an extended rear wing line. John Blatchley, senior styling engineer at Rolls-Royce, was responsible for the changes in design.

The Bentley has been taken to the Rolls-Royce London Service Centre for routine maintenance and possible rectification to the dent on the offside front wing, probably the result of a parking accident. Photographs were taken of all accident-damaged cars, not only to provide a visual account of the cars repaired, but as a record in the event of any subsequent customer or insurance enquiries.

This imposing photograph of an R-Type Bentley illustrates the extended rear wing line and lower wheel-arches which, with the longer boot, give added streamlining.

In the early post-war years British car manufacturers laid a great deal of emphasis on the export of motor vehicles to earn much-needed foreign currency. This Silver Dawn, embodying the modifications incorporated on the R-Type Bentley, is being carefully loaded aboard the *Empress of Australia* for a distant destination. The car has been prepared for shipping and, as well as its radiator, the front and rear bumpers are also shielded. In addition to having white wall tyres, this Rolls-Royce appears to have left-hand steering, which suggests the car may be on its way to America. It is worthy of note that throughout the United States the Bentley marque went mainly unnoticed and unrecognised. American customers appreciated only the prestige of the Rolls-Royce; its radiator shape and the Spirit of Ecstasy, as well as the car's ancestry, were wholly important.

Arriving at a Rolls-Royce Enthusiasts' meeting are these two Standard Steel saloons, the car nearest the camera a Sliver Dawn and the car behind it a Bentley Mk VI. Apart from the different styles of radiator, Silver Dawns could always be identified by their twin fog-lamps, whereas the Bentley featured just one, positioned centrally and immediately above bumper height. R-REC gatherings have always been grand affairs and attract enthusiasts from all over the world.

This photograph, taken in the early to mid-fifties, shows the spacious interior of the London Service Centre. Not only is it a model of efficiency but the cleanliness is clearly apparent. In the foreground a mechanic is getting to grips with a Mk VI Bentley, and note how carefully the car's paintwork is protected. Next to it, another Mk VI is having some extensive work carried out on it and the wings, bonnet and radiator have been removed. Further along the row of cars a Silver Wraith can be seen; look closely at the right-hand side of the picture where not only are some pre-war models receiving attention, but a couple of Bentley Continentals are in for service.

There is a hive of activity surrounding the Silver Wraith in the foreground and note also other cars in different stages of completion further away from the camera. The sheer size of the Silver Wraith is evident and it appears that it is being made ready for the fitment of trim items as well as the headlamps. To the right of the photographer is a Silver Dawn and behind it another Silver Wraith.

For those customers who demanded greater elegance and sophistication than a Standard Steel saloon could offer, specialist coachbuilders provided some breathtaking designs which included this magnificent Bentley. The styling is typical of that of H.J. Mulliner, the London coachbuilder, and the photographer has caught much of the careful detail for which the company was so famous. As would be expected, the interior finish of this car would complement the finery of the exterior.

The Rolls-Royce 40/50 Silver Ghost makes an interesting companion to the Silver Wraith, both models being the most prestigious cars available when introduced. Against the Silver Wraith, the size of the vintage car is easily discernible but, nevertheless, the corporate identity between the two vehicles has changed remarkably little. Note the headlamps, which are higher set on the Silver Wraith, and the radiator, which on the later car has shutters. For comfort and luxury there is little question as to which is the superior car; as to actually getting behind the wheel, that might be a different matter . . .

The classical styling of this Bentley R-Type with coachwork by James Young befits the car's surroundings of Kensington Gardens, a regular venue for Rolls-Royce and Bentley enthusiasts. This is a delightful picture, taken on a summer's day, and the elegance of the car, with its high-set headlamps and sweeping wing line, is typical of what was considered one of the world's most respected coachbuilders. Is it any wonder that the gentleman standing looking at the car appears to be captivated by its sheer beauty? The car's registration is significant in that the coachbuilder used JY, the letters which were reserved for Plymouth, and issued between March 1932 and February 1937.

This is the same car as that above; from the three-quarter rear view, the car appears just as elegant and the gentle wing line, together with the extended rear wings and wheel-arches, gives this car a fine sense of proportion. Note the discreet GB plate on the nearside rear wing, which is far more sophisticated than the modern stick-on version. Next to the Bentley is another coachbuilt car, possibly a Silver Wraith and, beyond that, a vintage Rolls-Royce. Taken on the same occasion as the photograph above, the group of Londoners appear to be enjoying the sight of so many fine cars gathered in a single location.

There was no greater admirer of Rolls-Royce than HH the Ruler of Kuwait who ordered this fine limousine with H.J. Mulliner coachwork on a Silver Wraith chassis. Close scrutiny will reveal this to be a Sedanca de Ville, and a feature of the car is its forward-hinged doors. Strangely, these cars appeared most elegant when the roof section over the chauffeur was in the open position.

There are few Rolls-Royces that could have been finished in a more distinctive manner than this Silver Wraith which was built for a Mr Webber. The simulated cane paintwork is strangely effective and does not appear totally out of place. The origin of the coachwork has the hallmark of being that of Freestone & Webb.

Another limousine built on the Silver Wraith chassis. The coachwork is Park Ward and has a very formal style about it. Note the half-enclosed wheel-arches, which give the car a somewhat heavy appearance, and the long sweeping front wings. The car has a gracefulness which is accentuated by the smooth rounded features, a departure from the semi-razor-edged styling so often seen on these vehicles.

Bearing the registration number YR 11, previously used on the Duke of Kent's Wraith, this H.J. Mulliner Silver Wraith was built for Princess Marina. A seven-passenger limousine, the car was constructed on the short wheelbase and, as a result, the boot appears somewhat stunted. As well as the royal crest, all royal cars had fitted a blue police lamp, which can be seen above the windscreen. The styling of the car appears rather formal but nevertheless typical of that specified by the royal family for ceremonial occasions.

Photographed at Buckingham Palace on a grey and misty autumn day, this ceremonial royal car makes a commanding picture. In formal style, the Phantom IV (chassis no. 4BP5), with its rear compartment hood lowered, has coachwork by Hooper. Note the police lamp, the royal crest and, instead of the Spirit of Ecstasy, the royal mascot.

With Princess Elizabeth sitting in the rear compartment, the first Phantom IV, which was hand-built at the Clan Foundry, near Belper, Derbyshire, elegantly makes its way past loyal and cheering crowds. The enclosed limousine, which has coachwork by H.J. Mulliner, was presented to Princess Elizabeth and the Duke of Edinburgh in July 1950 and it can be presumed this photograph was taken shortly afterwards.

The royal limousine, pictured from an unusual angle, can be seen leaving Buckingham Palace on what is clearly a ceremonial occasion. The sheer magnificence of the car is shown to good effect, the 12 foot 1 inch wheelbase being representative of the rationalised chassis in its fully stretched guise. In evidence is the transparent panel in the roof, which had an electrically operated interior cover. Additional equipment – which is not visible – includes an electrically powered rear blind, and an adjustable rear seat which, for ceremonial purposes, could be wound forward in order that their majesties could have a better view, as well as allowing spectators to see them more clearly.

Princess Elizabeth's limousine pictured before delivery to the royal family. A careful look at the radiator shell will reveal not the Spirit of Ecstasy but a mascot depicting St George slaying the Dragon. The police lamp can be seen above the windscreen and it was then customary, as now, for the royal car not to carry a registration plate. The exquisite styling, together with the extra wheelbase length, is shown to its best advantage in this specially prepared photograph.

HRH Princess Margaret took delivery of this magnificent Phantom IV in July 1954. The styling differed a little from the car that was delivered to Princess Elizabeth, in as much as it embodied a higher and more elongated wing line. This car also does not display the Spirit of Ecstasy but is fitted with a mascot depicting Pegasus, the winged horse. The photograph was taken in Belgrave Square, near Euston, and in the background can be seen a Bentley Mk VI. Some of the other vehicles are also of interest: furthest from the camera is a Standard Eight, in front of which is a Bedford van; approaching the photographer is a London taxicab, an Austin FX3, and parked against the railings is a Volkswagen Beetle. Next to it is a pre-war Standard with odd headlamps, one fitted lower than the other.

A close-up of Pegasus, the mascot fitted to Princess Margaret's Phantom IV. The highly polished radiator shell is very prominent and, by looking very carefully, the result of what the Greeks referred to as *entasis*, the practice they employed to make a surface look flat by giving it a slight convexity, is just discernible. As can be expected, the royal Phantom was most tastefully appointed; the rear seat could be adjusted for fore and aft movement and electrical controls operated the rear window blind, the central division and various interior lamps.

During the early fifties, Rolls-Royces gradually replaced Daimlers as royal cars. The Phantom IV, this example being the one delivered to HRH Princess Margaret in July 1954, was considered the finest car of its type available and was not supplied to any customer except royalty or heads of state. In total, just eighteen Phantom IVs were built.

H.J. Mulliner were not the only coachbuilders who prepared Phantom IVs. The vehicle pictured here, the second Phantom IV, was built by Park Ward, in-house coachbuilders to Rolls-Royce. It will be evident that there is something odd about the vehicle: note the twin side-mounted spare wheels without covers, and the style of coachwork which is barely visible. It is, in fact, a delivery truck and, as such, was used by Rolls-Royce as a company vehicle. Equipped with an automatic gearbox, it is claimed the top speed of this pick-up was over 90mph.

The Park Ward Phantom IV delivery truck revealed in profile, shown looking north from the Pyms Lane car park. Used not only as a works pick-up but as an experimental vehicle, this, without doubt, must have been one of the most unusual Rolls-Royces. The formidable power of this Phantom presented serious problems to the vehicle's drivers as, at the time of its construction, there was a 30mph limit for all commercials, of which this was most definitely an example. Surviving in the form photographed here, the Phantom was dismantled in 1963.

The profile of the Bentley Continental is as exciting as is its performance potential. This photograph of the prototype car demonstrates just how streamlined it is; there is little wonder that Evernden's design – with assistance from John Blatchley – provoked extreme adulation when unveiled in 1951. Almost immediately comparisons between this and the pre-war Corniche were being made, especially as initial plans had existed to name the model Corniche II. During tests, the car reached a speed of 114mph, using Dunlop medium-distance track tyres; the potential top speed was around 120mph, and this was achieved at Montlhéry. 'Olga', as the car became affectionately known, was used as a company demonstrator until 1960, by which time she had covered almost a quarter of a million miles.

A total of 208 R-Type Continental Bentleys were built between 1952 and 1955 and all, apart from fifteen, were constructed by H.J. Mulliner. Of those built by other coachbuilders, six were prepared by Park Ward, five by Franay in France and three by Graber in Switzerland. One car was built by Pininfarina. The Park Ward cars were styled by John Blatchley, Rolls-Royce's chief styling engineer. Among those customers who clamoured for a Bentley R-Type Continental were A.S. Onassis, Nicholas Monsarrat and Henry Ford.

Ivan Evernden's R-Type Continental is a model of aerodynamic efficiency. The two-door lightweight coachwork, by H.J. Mulliner, with full-width front wings and faired-in headlamps, caused a sensation when first seen; customers had to wait up to three years from placing an order to taking delivery. This car is a production model and differed from the prototype in a number of ways. As well as having a one-piece windscreen, production cars were equipped with a restyled facia, a one-inch higher roof-line and a radiator shell bearing the famous Bentley winged-B badge. It should be noted that the rear trim on this particular car was non-standard and some owners dispensed with the wheel spats altogether.

The R-Type Continental was conceived in 1950 and from the outset the aim had been to produce a sporting car much lighter in weight than the Standard Steel saloon. H.J. Mulliner had been responsible for building a lightweight saloon on the Bentley Mk VI chassis and, as the car embodied many of the features desired for the Continental, it was decided that the coachbuilder be asked to prepare a prototype. The result was a weight-cheating affair which utilised light alloy for the entire bodywork including the wings. Even the interior, which was superbly appointed, was designed to be weight-saving.

It is fitting that a picture of a Bentley R-Type Continental such as this should exist, if only to suggest the effect of streamlining which both the car and the de Havilland Comet achieved. Both machines were pioneers; the Comet for being the world's first commercial jet airliner and the Bentley for being the fastest production car available. Side by side, the two icons represent much more: not only did they both earn badly needed foreign currency but they symbolised the best that British technology and engineering could offer.

There can be hardly another car in the world that can share the charisma of the R-Type Bentley Continental. Arguably controversial in its styling, it is among the most sought-after of all Rolls-Royce and Bentley cars and pristine examples command high prices. Indeed, it is recognised as one of the world's great cars. The car's designer, Ivan Evernden, said of the Continental: 'After World War II, coachbuilders both at home and abroad made some very elegant bodies for the Bentley Mk VI chassis. But none possessed the total qualities of "Olga", for she evolved with a purpose, not only to look beautiful, but to exhibit those characteristics which appeal to the connoisseur of motoring; a high maximum road speed coupled with a correspondingly high rate of acceleration, together with excellent handling qualities and "roadability".'

'Olga' is in fact the prototype Continental, her name being derived simply from the registration number! Standing alongside is Ivan Evernden. The late Stanley Sedgwick, the respected authority on Bentley cars and founder of the Bentley Drivers' Club, owned 'Olga' for many years.

PASSING CLOUDS

Introduced in 1955, the Silver Cloud, on the right, and the Bentley S-Series, represented a new chapter in Rolls-Royce's standardisation programme. Both cars are pictured in front of the Crewe factory and the styling differences between the two models are clear. The Silver Cloud retains a more formal appearance while the Bentley, with its more curvaceous radiator styling, produces a softer expression and manages to convey more of a sporting flavour. Both models used the same engine and technology with automatic transmission as standard.

INTRODUCTION

The rationalisation programme which Rolls-Royce had embarked on in the late thirties and which produced the first post-war models was taken a step further towards standardising the Rolls-Royce and Bentley marques with the introduction of two new models, the Silver Cloud and Bentley S-Series, in 1955.

These cars were the work of John Blatchley, the eminent styling engineer who, in 1935, joined the respected coachbuilder Gurney Nutting and, two years later, at the age of twenty-three, was appointed that company's chief designer. At the outbreak of war, Blatchley was despatched to Rolls-Royce, not to style motor cars but to work on the design of aero-engine cowlings. Within four years of joining the motor car division under Ivan Evernden, John Blatchley was appointed chief styling engineer.

With the Silver Cloud's introduction, Rolls-Royce offered a Bentley version which, arguably, was less ostentatious and which appealed to more British customers than did its sister car. The Bentley, of course, was finished to exactly the same high specification as the Rolls-Royce, and thus created something of a syndrome which, for want of a better word, amounted to badge engineering.

As with their predecessors, the Silver Clouds were offered with Pressed Steel bodies: the Standard Steel saloon. Make no mistake, these cars were built to exemplary standards which were met with much enthusiasm and acclaim – but for those customers who insisted on bespoke coachwork, specialist coachbuilders were able to offer appropriately individual designs.

The engine which whispered along those graceful Silver Clouds was a 4,887cc version of the 6-cylinder IOE engine of the Silver Dawn and Bentley Mk VI which, in 1959, was superseded by a more powerful V8 of 6.2 litres capacity (6,230cc), a move which gave rise to the 'Series II' designation. Outwardly, the second generation cars appeared virtually identical to their predecessors but, apart from those under the bonnet, it was the modifications to the car's interior that were the most noticeable. Apart from a revised facia layout, there was a smaller steering wheel and some of the minor controls were redesigned.

The most obvious styling changes occurred in autumn 1962 with the introduction of the Silver Cloud III and Bentley S3. Along with a four-headlamp arrangement, the bonnet was lowered slightly in order to improve forward vision and the front wings were restyled; a new interior layout was also specified. For the purists, the Silver Cloud with its separate chassis remains representative of the final chapter in the development of the traditional Rolls-Royce.

The master at work! Chief styling engineer, John Blatchley, can be seen sculpting a quarter-scale model made from modelling clay. The design which John is carving is the Phantom V limousine which was introduced by Rolls-Royce in 1959. From a very early age John Blatchley developed the skill of designing motor cars, a skill which stood him in good stead when working with the coachbuilder Gurney Nutting.

The semi-razor-edged styling of the Silver Cloud is shown to good effect here and makes an interesting contrast to the contoured rear fuselage of the de Havilland Comet 4. Rolls-Royce made a point of having its cars photographed alongside aircraft, especially those which were specified as using its aero-engines.

The Vickers VC10, like the Comet, was another British landmark in aviation. Here, the aircraft, latterly favoured by the RAF, as well as by BOAC, which later, with BEA, became British Airways, symbolises the importance and prestige of British industry. Alongside the VC10 with its Rolls-Royce Conway engines, the imposing lines of the Silver Cloud rightly suggest the technical and engineering expertise for which the company was recognised. Introduced in 1955, the origins of the Silver Cloud's design can be traced to the immediate post-war era when a replacement for the Silver Dawn and Bentley Mk VI (and the R-Type) were first considered. Several designs were contemplated but rejected as too radical. Ultimately, the design that went into production was perceived as being the most appropriate and, in retrospect, was the correct choice.

The Silver Cloud was well received in America, from where this picture originates. Bearing a New York registration, the car is photographed alongside a Piedmont Airlines turbo-prop, a Fokker F27 built under licence by Fairchild. The significance of the illustration is, once again, Rolls-Royce's association with aviation and, in particular, with the company's aero-engine business. Under the bonnet of the Silver Cloud lies a straight-six power unit; the aircraft is propelled by Rolls-Royce Dart engines.

As well as a Standard Steel saloon, the Silver Cloud was available, from 1957, with a longer wheelbase. Company literature described this as being a dual-purpose car, designed to cater for the executive who used the car during the week on business, driven by a chauffeur, and at weekends or on holiday, when the owner would drive the car.

There could hardly be a more evocative photograph of a Bentley S-Series than this; the full extent of the car's gracefulness and poise is captured by the camera and, of course, is enhanced by the quintessentially English surroundings.

The Silver Cloud and its Bentley equivalent were important export commodities for Rolls-Royce and for Britain. In this photograph a left-hand drive Bentley S1 is being gently loaded aboard the SS *Brandager*. As to its destination and eventual customer, that is not clear but the white wall tyres suggest the USA.

Pictured in Stockholm at a trade convention, this Bentley convertible is earning business for both Rolls-Royce and Britain. As well as the delectable lines of the car, there is much to see: note the Volvo P44, the Ford Popular behind it and, on the extreme left, a split-screen Volkswagen Transporter.

In 1959, a second-generation Silver Cloud was introduced. Although it appeared almost identical to the model it replaced, it nevertheless featured a new engine, a V8. A little over 6 litres in capacity, the power unit was notable in as much as it managed to pack into a length slightly less than that of the in-line engine, another 1½ litres, producing something like 30 per cent greater output. This was the mainstay of Rolls-Royce motor cars for a number of years and was fitted, in an updated form, to the Silver Shadow and Bentley T-Series. With its revision of power, the Silver Cloud was redesignated Silver Cloud II, a similar nomenclature being awarded to the Bentley, which became the S2, an example of which is seen here.

An important facet of motor car design and production at Rolls-Royce was the company's commitment to continual improvement, which meant that the experimental department was kept constantly busy. This photograph, taken outside the experimental garage at the Crewe factory, is of a Bentley S-Series car which has been adapted to test crosswind stability, the massive tail fins having been fitted for the purpose. A close look at the photograph reveals that the Bentley appears to be rather battle-scarred, a result, no doubt, of many hours and thousands of miles of rigorous testing.

Possibly one of the most unusual variants of the Silver Cloud is this Rolls-Royce Town and Country estate car which is one of four specially built, two having been prepared on the standard wheelbase chassis and a further two on the longer wheelbase. All four cars featured left-hand drive, and incorporated body modifications by H.J. Mulliner; the interior work was carried out by Harold Radford, the south-west London coachbuilder recognised for its estate car conversions on a wide range of vehicles.

The appointment of the Town and Country estate cars, one of which was displayed at the 1959 New York Motor Show, was of very high quality. The rear seats were made to fold forward to allow unrestricted space behind the front seats, and access to the rear compartment could be gained through the split tailgate. In addition to the estate models, Harold Radford also offered a Countryman conversion based on the standard saloon which, as well as featuring a Webasto sun roof, specified luxury fittings that included a drinks cabinet, picnic requisites and even an electric kettle and a washing bowl.

Of all the coachbuilt Silver Clouds, few could rival this James Young Sedanca, based on the Silver Cloud II long-wheelbase chassis, for sheer elegance. Note the hooded headlamps, the rear wing extensions which house the tail lamps and the rear-hinged rear doors, a feature synonymous with this style of coachwork. The incongruous surroundings are in stark contrast to the car's majestic lines but nevertheless produce an effect which is strangely attractive.

Twin headlamps and a slightly lower bonnet line were features of the third and final series of Silver Clouds and S-Series cars when introduced in 1962. Pictured outside the main entrance to the Crewe factory, the styling modifications are plain to see on this Silver Cloud III. At the same time, similar revisions were made to the Bentley, which was designated the S3. Not only did the new lighting arrangement provide better road illumination, but the lower radiator shell with a correspondingly steeper slope of the bonnet improved forward vision. As a consequence of this restyling, the front wings were reshaped and the side lamps were repositioned, together with flashing indicators, in the wing's leading edge. Modifications to the car's interior applied mainly to the facia and the front seats, the latter providing added comfort and lateral support.

Unlike the Phantom IV, which was specified purely for royalty and heads of state, the Phantom V, introduced in 1959, was offered, like all Rolls-Royce cars, to special order. Built on a lengthened Silver Cloud II chassis, the Phantom V provided the ultimate in spacious refinement and performance.

The Phantom VI was introduced on 1 January 1969, by which time the Silver Shadow had been in production for a little over three years. It was a development of the Phantom V and featured a number of significant modifications including twin air-conditioning units, one for the front compartment, the other serving the rear.

OUT OF THE SHADOW

In the heart of London, outside Wine Office Court, this Silver Shadow makes for a particularly elegant study. It is little wonder that demand for the car quickly exceeded supply and waiting lists began to lengthen. Not surprisingly, previously used Silver Shadows sold for considerable sums. Compared to the Silver Cloud, the Silver Shadow appealed to a wider clientele who, as well as being owner drivers, also tended to be younger. In the background, parked adjacent to the building under construction, can be seen a British Road Services lorry, which were usually Bristols, a once-familiar sight on the roads of Britain!

INTRODUCTION

When introduced in autumn 1965, the Silver Shadow and its Bentley equivalent, the T-Series, represented for Rolls-Royce a huge forward leap in technology.

Understandably there were those who mourned Rolls-Royce's decision to meet a changing climate in the needs of a motoring clientele head-on. However, had Rolls-Royce believed they could have survived by producing the most exclusive of cars in modestly low numbers, the company would surely have gone out of business. Because of the demise of the specialist coachbuilder, brought about by the need to produce greater numbers of cars more cheaply, Rolls-Royce's engineers accepted the formidable challenge of using modern motor engineering methods which included adopting unitary construction. The alternative was unthinkable.

The genesis of the Silver Shadow can be traced to the mid-fifties. It was during this period that Harry Grylls, chief engineer at Rolls-Royce, conceived the type of car that would take the company forward, over two decades, the sixties and seventies.

Although still an embryonic concept, the full extent of Grylls's ideas did not materialise until the late fifties when development work on the then current cars, the Silver Cloud and Bentley S, was almost complete. Only then was the full scale of the project, which entailed the design and development of a motor vehicle quite different in concept from anything previously produced by the company, realised. The Silver Shadow evolved from two quite different design projects, one a Rolls-Royce and known within the company by its project name, 'Tibet', the other a Bentley, referred to as 'Burma'. The costs, not only purely monetary but directly related to the number of man-hours required to perfect what was a most radical and technically advanced motor car to the standards expected of a Rolls-Royce, were, understandably, enormous.

Few could have envisaged at the time of introduction that the Silver Shadow would have a production span of fifteen years and that the Corniche, a development of the Mulliner Park Ward two-door model, would survive well into the nineties. Few, furthermore, would have guessed at the car's popularity which resulted in its being built in (comparatively) huge numbers. Including the Camargue, a very special if controversial derivative of the Silver Shadow, production amounted to over 40,500 vehicles, which says much for the success of Rolls-Royce's perception of exactly what its customers wanted.

The architect of the Silver Shadow was Harry Grylls, chief engineer at Rolls-Royce from 1951 until 1968, the year he retired from the company after thirty-eight years' service. The picture was taken outside the main entrance to the Crewe factory and the car, wearing a registration number reserved for publicity vehicles, is one of the first Silver Shadows to be built. In October 1965 *Motor* described the Silver Shadow as 'almost certainly the best and quite certainly the most sophisticated car in the world'. Without doubt the Silver Shadow – and the Bentley T – was Grylls's finest achievement; from the time initial outline plans were laid in 1954, development of the car took eleven years although, due to design work currently under way with the Silver Cloud, serious engineering considerations did not begin until the late fifties. It was Harry Grylls's foresight and engineering expertise which not only ensured the Silver Shadow was a resounding success, but whose direction and engineering policies formed the substance of Rolls-Royce motor cars for following generations.

Silver Shadow was the name given to the Silver Cloud's successor. Although some consideration had been given to the project as early as 1954, it was not until 1958, when production of the Silver Cloud and Bentley S-Series cars was well established, that serious design work was possible. The 'Tibet' was to incorporate chassisless (monocoque or unitary) construction techniques for the first time in Rolls-Royce production. The reason for the change in production methods was dictated by several factors – mainly that it was no longer possible to maintain production quantities because of the limits imposed on the coachbuilding industry in view of its state of terminal decline. Changes in the motor industry and customer perceptions also dictated that cars should be smaller by design; by building the platform and body together as a single unit it was possible to reduce a car's external dimensions without any loss whatsoever in the amount of interior space.

Under the direction of John Blatchley, senior stylist at Rolls-Royce, a scale model of Tibet II is being crafted on a modelling table by stylist Martin Bourne. The measuring bridge and grid is clearly evident and the definitive Silver Shadow shape can be clearly seen although, at this stage of the design work, the intention was for a larger vehicle than that eventually introduced. Note the distance between the front wheel-arch and the door which, in the production car, was rather less than shown here. The model does give some indication of how the car evolved, via 'Burma', as the Silver Shadow.

Three generations of Rolls-Royces are depicted in this photograph, taken in the experimental garage at the Crewe factory. The Tibet prototype can be seen on the right while to the left of it is a Silver Cloud and, on the far left, a Silver Dawn, the first Rolls-Royce to be equipped with a Standard Steel body. Although Tibet was the first stage in the Silver Shadow's ultimate development, the definitive shape is clearly evident. Note the indicators on the top leading edges of the front wings, the styling of which was subsequently altered. An interesting point is the shape and dimensions of the radiator which, instead of being rather tall as on other post-war models, returned to something like that fitted to the original cars, i.e. the long axis returned to the horizontal.

Testing of the experimental Tibet cars, of which the vehicle shown was the first, was, by necessity, a prolonged and complicated affair. 5 ELG was completed in August 1958 and made its maiden run shortly after. While the car experienced a good standard of ride, it suffered from severe vibration, excessive roll when cornering, and tight steering. To conceal the car's identity or heritage, most of the testing was conducted using a non-Rolls-Royce radiator and with a complete lack of badging. The car illustrated remained at the experimental garage until the autumn of 1962 when it was dismantled.

This side profile of Tibet, photographed in the experimental garage at the Crewe factory, demonstrates the relatively close design between this, the first prototype car designed as a replacement for the Silver Cloud, and the definitive Silver Shadow. The length between the front wheel-arch and the door can be seen to good effect as can the overall wheelbase which, in the Burma project (aimed initially at designing a new Bentley) was shortened by some 6½ inches. Several other features are also evident in this picture: note the styling treatment of the rear quarter panel, the high-mounted rear indicators and curved windscreen and the peak above it, a current styling trend found on several popular models of the day. Curved glass for windscreens was a recent advance when this prototype car was built, as glass manufacturers at that time were only beginning to develop the experience and technology that exists today. Large-section bumpers have been fitted at the front; there do not appear to be any at the rear.

Not only was the first Tibet experimental car the first Rolls-Royce to be constructed using a monocoque body shell, it also employed the use of air suspension. During tests, the suspension had a habit of leaking air overnight and had to be pumped up each morning before trials could begin. During its four years of evaluation, this most radical of Rolls-Royces provided company engineers with much technological information.

Soon after the Tibet project had got under way, work began on the development of an altogether smaller car, the Burma, which was to have been marketed as a Bentley. Much of the work on this and Tibet was carried out in parallel and eventually the two projects were merged. From then on, the car destined as the Silver Shadow followed more closely the Burma design although many features from Tibet were adopted. In this picture of a prototype Burma 3, photographed outside the experimental garage at Crewe, the resemblance between this and the definitive model can be appreciated – apart from the radiator styling. Note how the wings have been reshaped to incorporate newly defined indicators, a feature previously seen on the Silver Cloud III and Bentley S3 but modified slightly so that the top of the lamp unit was set in. The roof line was also altered to eliminate the peak above the windscreen, which alone reduced the drag by 4 per cent, and the wheelbase is shorter than that on the Tibet. Look carefully at the rear quarter panel: although still reminiscent of that seen on Tibet, it was subsequently altered.

It was at the Le Mans circuit in France that the pre-war Bentleys achieved so much success and it is therefore hardly surprising that it was to that venue that this experimental Bentley Burma prototype returned to undergo endurance testing. Pictured alongside the pits is the same car illustrated on the previous page and, by looking carefully, the test driver, John Gaskell, can just be seen standing on the barrier behind the car. It is a matter of interest that detailed logs relating to the exhaustive tests carried out on all experimental cars have been carefully retained by Rolls-Royce in company archives. Owners of Rolls-Royce and Bentley cars may also be interested to know that manufacturing and test details of every car built exist, and a copy may be obtained from the Rolls-Royce Enthusiasts' Club.

This Burma prototype car is undergoing trials at Le Mans. John Gaskell, a member of Rolls-Royce's test-driving team, takes a welcome break from the tedious task of making countless laps of the circuit. Not all the tests were carried out at Le Mans; many thousands of miles were covered throughout France on the Routes Nationales, as well as in other parts of Europe. Extensive trials were also conducted in America and Canada. In tests which were conducted over 18 months, some 71,000 miles were recorded, the majority of them with John Gaskell at the wheel. By comparing this photograph with the previous picture, some subtle differences between the two cars, of which this is an earlier example, will be apparent, namely the mesh-type grille and a slightly different headlamp arrangement. It should be noted that both the grille and headlamps were designed purely for experimental purposes and were not intended for fitment to production cars.

A number of experimental studies during the sixties provided the Rolls-Royce design team with a lot of information, but not all prototype cars materialised into specific models. The car photographed here is such an example and depicts a particularly attractive and graceful sports car. Given the code-name Korea, the car was styled by V. Koren and would, had it been adopted, have resulted in a high-performance machine with a maximum speed of around 133mph.

Wilhelm Koren's interior styling of his 133mph coupé clearly shows the progressive design he attributed to the Korea project. Note the impressive veneer facia and the comprehensive instrumentation, all in the finest Bentley tradition.

During the sixties there existed a collaboration between Rolls-Royce and the British Motor Corporation which was seeking to produce a car in the luxury segment of the market. Rolls-Royce had also agreed to an exchange of ideas that could have resulted in the development of a smaller Bentley. The coalition was ill-fated and there was only one prototype car from Crewe, code-named Java and pictured here.

The testing of every Rolls-Royce model is a very necessary and important part of the company's production policy. Martin Bourne, who at the time was a 'young' styling engineer at Crewe, is shown taking a rest and enjoying a mineral water while en route to Geneva. The left-hand drive car was being taken to Switzerland to be used for demonstration purposes during the Geneva Motor Show.

Undergoing this sort of treatment proves beyond all doubt the strengths and weaknesses of any car, Rolls-Royce included. In this scene, which was pictured at MIRA, the motor industry's proving centre, a car is about to be examined following a controlled side-impact test. Rolls-Royce's engineers were usually very good at economising on their test cars, to the extent that they could often get up to four crashes out of a single vehicle. The force of this crash has resulted in the deformation of the monocoque shell which has had the effect of pushing the roof upwards and of compressing the passenger compartment. Considering the build quality of the Silver Shadow, the effect of the crash is obvious to see. The other cars in the scene include a BMC 1800, two Ford Cortinas, an estate car and a saloon, and in the distance a Jaguar.

Two generations of Rolls-Royces are visible in this photograph, taken on the day the Silver Shadow was unveiled to the company's agents and dealerships. Alongside the Silver Shadow which is wearing the registration 100 LG, a plate reserved for publicity cars, is a Silver Cloud. The twin headlamps reveal this as a Silver Cloud III, the final development in a range of cars that was first introduced in 1955. The Silver Shadow's monocoque construction enabled stylists and designers to produce a car of considerably lesser dimensions than its predecessor while improving interior room and comfort.

At the time that the Silver Shadow was launched, a Bentley equivalent was also unveiled. The T-Series Bentley was identical to the Rolls-Royce in all but radiator styling and badging. The price was marginally lower, by about £60, which meant that the majority of customers preferred to pay a minimal premium in order to have what was considered by some to be the more prestigious name and emblem. For enthusiasts of the Bentley marque, however, nothing other than a car sporting the 'winged B' emblem was good enough. In this photograph, members of Rolls-Royce dealerships, along with factory personnel, who had gathered at Crewe to see the unveiling of the new Rolls-Royce and Bentley, prepare to depart for a familiarisation run.

At the dealer launch of the Silver Shadow and Bentley T, which was held at the Crewe factory over two days, 30 September–1 October 1965, the managing director of Rolls-Royce Motor Cars, Dr F. Llewellyn-Smith, explains some of the latter car's finer points to his wife. Also in the picture is Fred Murray and, on his left, J. Macraith Fisher. Jack Phillips, chief of engine design, has his back to the camera. Following this event the cars were despatched to France in time for the Paris Motor Show, where the models were officially unveiled.

The Silver Shadow and Bentley T made their official British debut at the 1965 London Motor Show. Pictured at Earls Court, where the Silver Shadow deservedly attracted huge attention, the car is displayed minus its doors, a very unusual practice for Rolls-Royce. The reason for this was to demonstrate the benefits of unitary construction and to disprove any rumours that a car smaller in external dimensions than its predecessors had less interior space. Where other manufacturers often displayed their cars in such a state of 'undress', to denude a Rolls-Royce in this fashion had previously been considered rather lacking in taste.

This early publicity photograph shows the Bentley T in its definitive form. Evolution of both the Silver Shadow and its Bentley equivalent had taken eleven years, although much of the serious styling and design did not begin until the late fifties. The new generation of cars bristled with technology: as well as employing chassisless construction, a completely new production technique as far as Rolls-Royce was concerned, the models incorporated self-levelling hydraulic suspension in addition to the more conventional road springs. One of the reasons for adopting this novel suspension was to provide a completely even and comfortable ride which would not have been fully possible using conventional techniques. The quality of the new cars was every bit as expected; only the finest hides, veneers and carpeting were chosen while, on the mechanical side, endless care and effort was taken to ensure that the final product performed to the satisfaction of a fastidious customer.

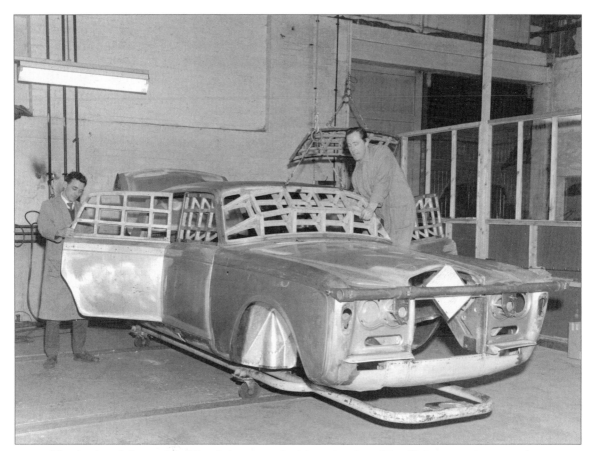

The demise of the coachbuilding industry resulted in a situation of insufficient capacity to produce bespoke coachwork in the quantities needed to satisfy Silver Shadow production, so body shells were produced by Pressed Steel at Cowley, Oxford. From there they were delivered to Rolls-Royce at Crewe where a specially designed production plant had been established to accommodate the entire build process. In its unpainted state as shown here, the shell was referred to as 'body in white' and, on arrival at Crewe, was given an exhaustive inspection to check for imperfections. All the initial checks, a process which included adapting for either left- or right-hand steering, took two days to be carried out.

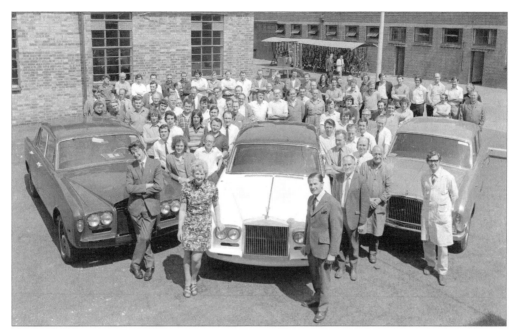

Just how many people did it take to build a Rolls-Royce Silver Shadow? A lot more than the group pictured here who represent the road test personnel at Crewe! At the forefront is Norman Bentley, the department's manager when this picture was taken on 17 June 1973.

One of the company demonstrators photographed in London, near Marble Arch. The car's suspension system was designed to cope with all types of road surface, from city streets like these to those found in the outback of Australia, for example. The Silver Shadow was particularly favoured by American customers who were used to cars with soft springing, such as the Cadillac.

Although the coachbuilding industry had declined greatly by the time the Silver Shadow was introduced, Rolls-Royce was nevertheless able to offer two-door coachbuilt versions of both this and the Bentley. These cars, both in fixed-head and convertible form, were produced by Mulliner Park Ward, a subsidiary of Rolls-Royce. The build process was a complicated affair. The platforms were delivered by Pressed Steel direct to the London coachbuilder where the body shells were constructed. Then the body shells were despatched to Crewe where they received their sub-frames and mechanical components before being returned to Mulliner Park Ward for paint and trim. Not surprisingly these cars attracted a hefty price premium which amounted to something like 50 per cent over that of the four-door saloon models.

The two-door models were styled in-house by John Blatchley, senior stylist, and Bill Allen, his deputy. It is possible to note in this picture the 'retro' styling introduced for the Mulliner Park Ward cars which amounted to a graceful lift of the wing line above the rear wheel. The rationale behind this exercise was to create a link with some of the earlier post-war Rolls-Royce and Bentley coachbuilt models. In 1971 the two-door models were substantially revised and renamed Corniche, again a name intended to revive memories of pre-war Bentleys.

The 'retro' styling theme of the two-door models is particularly evident in this photograph which depicts the Mulliner Park Ward convertible. The first of the two-door cars, the fixed-head coupé, was launched just six months after the introduction of the Silver Shadow, but customers had to wait until 1967 for the convertible. Below the waistline, both cars were identical; above it, the convertible was fitted with a hood that was both designed and built by Mulliner Park Ward. Despite the price difference between these and the standard saloons, the two-door models were eagerly sought after.

The two-door Silver Shadow models were built in both Rolls-Royce and Bentley versions, the latter of which is shown in this photograph. The convertible was particularly sought after in America, where it was especially appreciated by Californians whose climate allowed them to enjoy open-top motoring for much of the year. An integral feature of the two-door models was the smooth General Motors automatic gearbox which, along with the self-levelling suspension and powered steering, offered the ultimate in ride quality. Particularly noticeable here is the gentle uplift of the car's waistline, the Bentley monogram on the wheel hub caps, and the slim, unobtrusive door handles. The hood, in the lowered position, is also relatively inconspicuous.

The car pictured here represents a milestone in the history of the Silver Shadow, for it is the ten thousandth car to have been produced. Having received the keys to his car, the proud owner is about to take delivery. Sadly, the identity of the gentleman is unknown. The familiar radiator is seen to good effect and it is interesting to note that the radiator shell is not in fact built with flat surfaces as the picture suggests. A careful look at a Rolls-Royce radiator will reveal that the surfaces are very slightly curved. A further close look at the radiator will reveal that it has a slight forward inclination.

As well as the Mulliner Park Ward cars, James Young, the respected Bromley, Kent, coachbuilder, also offered a two-door version of the Silver Shadow. The James Young cars actually pre-dated those produced by Mulliner Park Ward and the difference in styling between the two versions is clearly evident. Notice that in this picture of a James Young vehicle, the waistline is identical to that found on the Silver Shadow saloons produced at Crewe and does not have the uplift of Mulliner Park Ward cars. As a coachbuilder, James Young did not have the resources that the Rolls-Royce subsidiary company enjoyed and the only way they could offer this variant was to buy a complete car from Crewe before carrying out the conversion. The extent of the customisation was mainly cosmetic and included modifying the door pillars and fitting new doors. Only 50 James Young two-door cars were built, 35 of which were Rolls-Royces and the remaining 15 Bentleys. The project was abandoned in 1967 due to few orders having been received, a situation which was no doubt exacerbated by the huge price premium imposed on these cars for what amounted to minimum visual differences from the standard car. Shortly after the abandonment of the project James Young went out of business. This was a sad end to what was a very highly respected coachbuilder.

As well as producing a fixed-head coupé and a convertible based on the Silver Shadow, Rolls-Royce offered a long-wheelbase saloon which was also built in conjunction with Mulliner Park Ward. The car shown in this photograph was specially built for HRH Princess Margaret and it is possible to see the royal coat of arms, together with the police lamp, above the windscreen. The specification of this car complied with Princess Margaret's specific requirements and included a dark green paint finish and matching green hide trim. The carpets were of pale grey-green and the facia was made from oiled teak. The princess also specified a rear seat that had both height and forward adjustment, which was useful for ceremonial occasions, leather door cappings instead of the more usual burr walnut, and a satin finish to all brightwork.

Long-wheelbase saloons had an extra 4 inches added to the floorpan and bodyshells were delivered to Mulliner Park Ward in London where the conversion was carried out. Once this part of the work was complete, the car was sent to Crewe for finishing.

R. Allwright stands with the two cars in his life, a Silver Shadow and Silver Cloud. The difference in size between the two cars is clear, the monocoque construction of the Silver Shadow allowing for just as much interior comfort as the Silver Cloud. The Silver Shadow's self-levelling suspension, along with its conventional coil springing, helped produce a ride of such quality that it was second to none.

In 1970 Ray Richards, along with Bill Bengry and David Skeffington, who acted as navigator, entered this Silver Shadow in the *Daily Mirror* London to Mexico Marathon. The car, which was substantially modified for the rally, was fitted with a crash bar, and the exhaust was re-routed from its usual under-car position, through the bonnet and across the roof to terminate above the rear window.

John Blatchley and his styling team were considering a number of design modifications for a second series Silver Shadow. This is a full-size mock-up of a car that never went into production, but a careful look at the photograph will reveal several interesting points such as the rubber overriders on the front bumper (never a feature on Series I cars), reflectors and side repeaters on the front wings, and a side reflector on the rear wings. The rear quarter panels and boot line are quite different from those on the production model.

This is the prototype second-series Silver Shadow, this time photographed from the rear. The most obvious change concerns the styling of the rear window, quarter panel and boot. Note the rear lamp design which is also quite different from that on production cars. The boot styling is somewhat reminiscent of some US cars of the period and, oddly, appears to be rather advanced in that a number of manufacturers, both American and Japanese, adopted a similar style during the 1980s. John Blatchley claims not to have been enamoured with this design.

Pictured on the sports field of the Pyms Lane factory at Crewe, the prototype second-series car can be seen along with a Silver Shadow saloon, on the left, and a Silver Cloud III, on the extreme right. The differences in style between the production Silver Shadow and the design study are clearly evident, most noticeable being the rear treatment of the car. The project was eventually abandoned. An interesting detail about this picture is the American car, a front-wheel drive Oldsmobile Toronado, which Rolls-Royce was then evaluating. It was not unusual for Rolls-Royce, or another manufacturer, to obtain different cars with the aim of taking them apart for investigative purposes. John Blatchley, the epitome of an English gentleman, had, somewhat surprisingly, a very high regard for American cars and no doubt would have been highly interested in the Oldsmobile.

When it was introduced in 1977, the revised version of the Silver Shadow, the Silver Shadow II, appeared with external modifications that were mostly cosmetic. It was under the bonnet that most of the changes were made. Apart from redesigned bumpers and a discreet badge on the boot lid, the Silver Shadow II was remarkably reminiscent of the earlier cars – but look carefully at the radiator and it can be seen that the shell is marginally deeper than before. The grilles below the headlamps have also been deleted and below the bumper an air-dam, to aid straight line stability, was fitted along with carefully concealed fog lamps. It will be noticed that the car depicted has been fitted with headlamp washers, a feature which identifies this as a late model. Series II cars were fitted with a split-level automatic air-conditioning system which, once set, kept the passenger compartment at a constant temperature. A Series II Silver Shadow can also be identified by its facia, which underwent considerable restyling.

Changes to the Silver Shadow resulting in the Series II designation were also applied to the Bentley, which became the T2. The car, wearing a number plate used for publicity purposes, is pictured outside the London premises of the Lobb company, famous for its shoes. In relation to the Silver Shadow, the Bentley was produced in relatively few numbers, total production being less than 7 per cent of the equivalent Rolls-Royce.

The Italian coachbuilder Pininfarina produced this interesting Bentley coupé in 1968. It was built around the Silver Shadow platform and although the styling was somewhat controversial it nevertheless was generally reminiscent of the Bentley Continentals that were so revered when introduced a decade earlier. Photographed at the 1968 Earls Court Motor Show, this was the sole car produced in this style; although the rectangular headlamps were by no means elegant, the car did possess a certain panache, especially with its fastback styling and unmistakable Italian flair. The car was built for James (now Lord) Hanson, the well-known industrialist and financier.

The Pininfarina Bentley T must have made an impression, for it was not long after the car's unveiling that the Italian stylist was invited by Rolls-Royce to produce a two-door coupé of such design and proportion that it would be hailed as the company's flagship. The brief that Pininfarina received from Rolls-Royce was that the car had to offer even greater luxury than either the current Silver Shadow or the Mulliner Park Ward models. The design that emerged from Pininfarina was altogether different from the car shown at the 1968 London Motor Show; for all its impressive size the Camargue, as it became known, followed much in the way of contemporary Italian styling trends and as soon as it was unveiled, in January 1975, became the subject of continual contention and debate among Rolls-Royce enthusiasts.

In this photograph, taken at the time of the Camargue's introduction, the proportions of the car can be easily understood. When seen against a Silver Shadow, the bulk of the Camargue is very noticeable and it is well known that Pininfarina was presented with some problems in arriving at a satisfactory style in keeping with the traditional Rolls-Royce radiator. The interior of the Camargue was beautifully appointed with the softest Nuela hide; the facia and instruments, which were specially designed by Pininfarina, acknowledged Rolls-Royce's long association with aviation. The Camargue enjoyed a certain exclusiveness and when introduced was recognised as being the most expensive car in the British catalogue – which probably explains why just 530, including a single car badged as a Bentley, were built.

Apart from providing a clear illustration of the Camargue, the photograph also depicts the fashions of the mid-seventies; as well as the trendy London mews scene, note the gentleman's suave attire, complete with flares!

In 1971 the Official Receiver was appointed to take over the administration of Rolls-Royce following a débâcle concerning the company's aero-engine interests. It is, however, important to stress that Rolls-Royce was never bankrupt, as is the popular misconception. A few weeks later the Corniche, which was a development of the two-door Mulliner Park Ward cars, was introduced and received with much acclaim. In view of the publicity surrounding the Rolls-Royce affair, launching the Corniche at that time was seen as something of a fillip for the company, especially as the car offered the ultimate in performance and luxury. Both fixed-head coupé and convertible versions were available until 1980, after which only the latter, as seen here, remained listed in the Rolls-Royce catalogue. Even today it is possible to specify a car built to special order on application to the manufacturer.

Outside the main entrance to the Rolls-Royce factory at Crewe in early 1996, the last production Corniche is pictured with just some of the stylists, designers, engineers and test drivers who worked on the Silver Shadow programme during the fifties, sixties and seventies. Although the Corniche is no longer officially included in the Rolls-Royce catalogue it is still available to special order. No prices are quoted as each car made is costed individually.

Standing behind the car, left to right, are: Martin Bourne; Roger Cra'ster; Eric Langley; John Astbury; Bill Allen; George Ray; John Cooke. In the foreground are: Derek Coulson; John Gaskell; J. (Mac) Macraith Fisher; Jock Knight.

EPILOGUE

The flagship of the Rolls-Royce range is the Park Ward limousine and, as such, it recalls a name which again has a special position in Rolls-Royce and Bentley history. The model's turbocharged engine has been designed to afford a 25 per cent increase in power and, as is expected of such a delectable carriage, the refinement is nothing less than exquisite. Production of this car is limited to no more than 20 per year.

INTRODUCTION

The era of the Silver Shadow had been a tempestuous one; not only did it signal fundamental changes in the manner in which Rolls-Royce motor cars were to be built and marketed, but it also raised fears that the company, which had become something of a national institution, was as vulnerable to market forces as any other business. It was also a period when the Bentley marque's light was almost – but not quite – hidden under the Rolls-Royce bushel to the extent that it almost disappeared into obscurity. Sales of the Bentley T, compared to those of the Silver Shadow, reached a low of 3 per cent and, had the marque been allowed to drop quietly into oblivion, that act would have been one of the saddest – and one of the most deplorable – in the history of the motor car.

The Silver Spirit was designed as a car very much for the eighties and nineties and its introduction, in the autumn of 1980, was viewed as particularly auspicious. A new model in the Rolls-Royce range is always an event but, on this occasion, the importance was heightened by its coinciding with the company's merger with Vickers plc. The Silver Spirit was a much more modern car than the model it replaced: its styling was more angular, which made it appear appreciably larger when in fact it was only 3 inches longer and 2 inches wider, and its glass area was also greater, by a third. A long-wheelbase car, the Silver Spur, was also offered and, for the Bentley enthusiast, there was the Mulsanne. Rolls-Royce deliberately set out to restore the Bentley marque to something approaching its former glory and, while the Mulsanne saw a revival in sales, it was the Mulsanne Turbo, introduced in 1982, that was to have a dramatic effect on the car's latter-day recognition as a luxury performance car.

From its derisory 3 per cent of the company market, Bentley sales quickly grew thanks to a whole new marketing strategy which included the Bentley Eight, a carefully priced car that was introduced in 1984 and which was aimed specifically at attracting customers who might well not previously have considered Rolls-Royce or Bentley ownership. This was the car that featured a mesh grille, so recapturing the sporting image for which the marque was so famous, together with a slightly reduced level of trim but without loss of any comfort or handling quality.

There is nowhere in the world that the cars from Crewe are not revered; not only is each customer considered very special, but also evident within the company to this day y Royce himself.

olls-Royce and Bentley enjoys an ancestry which is unique and as been portrayed in the pages and photographs of this book. On an older Rolls-Royce is seen on the road, there exists for the ment which no amount of media publicity could possibly better.

When introduced in 1980, the Silver Spirit range of cars replaced the Silver Shadow II and the Silver Wraith II. The Corniche Convertible and Camargue, an example of which is illustrated on the left, remained in production. The Silver Spirit was designed around the Silver Shadow II's platform, engine and transmission, but utilised the rear suspension which had first been devised for the Camargue and Corniche models a year earlier. The car on the right is, in fact, a Silver Spur, the long-wheelbase version of the Silver Spirit.

Bentley enthusiasts who no longer had the T-Series car from which to choose were offered the Mulsanne, although the Corniche was marketed until 1984 when it was renamed the Continental. In this form it remained in the catalogue until 1995, after which it could be specified to special order only.

For 1997, the Silver Spur received the benefit of light pressure turbocharging which provided a performance increase of some 25 per cent. Further modifications included a revised security system and heated rear seats. To meet customers' requirements, an optional entertainment system together with a refrigerator and cocktail requisites were offered.

Introduced as a new model, the Silver Dawn recaptures the spirit of a past era; designed to feature all the benefits of the Silver Spirit, it is powered by a normally aspirated engine and has a further 4 inches added to the rear passenger compartment, as in the Silver Spur. The Silver Dawn is available in short-wheelbase form when it is badged as the Silver Spirit.

Bentley sales now comprise more than half of all vehicle production, a massive increase since the sixties and seventies. To a great extent, the Bentley marque is following a separate course and offers customers the ultimate in technology and design together with a performance that is commensurate with the marque's history. The Bentley Brooklands, a name strongly associated with the marque's racing history, is equipped with a turbocharger which pushes the car's output to 300bhp.

The Bentley Turbo R, with its liquid-cooled intercooler, produces 385bhp; a longer wheelbase is now standard on these cars, although the shorter-wheelbase model, as ever, remains available to special order.

The Bentley Continental R enjoys a particular styling which is reminiscent of the earlier Continentals and the Corniche. The bristling technology of this car includes micro alloy brakes and electronic traction assistance systems, both of which are also specified for the Turbo R and Continental T. The car's interior is rather different from that normally expected of the marque and captures very successfully the grand sporting appeal that was essentially the hallmark of the pre-Derby Bentleys.

The Continental T is possibly the most remarkable performance car available today. With a concept of style that has been applied to the Continental R, this is the true long-distance touring machine with a formidable performance. Enhanced by its electronic transient boost control, which effectively overrides the normal maximum boost of the turbocharger, especially when overtaking or when a sudden surge of power is required, the responsiveness of this car is phenomenal.

The ultimate sporting Bentley is the Azure. This is a convertible edition of the Continental R which was developed with the co-operation of Pininfarina. When introduced in March 1995 at the Geneva Motor Show, Rolls-Royce claimed that it was the most exciting product announcement in recent years. Undoubtedly W.O. Bentley would have approved, as would C.S. Rolls and Henry Royce.

INDEX